MORE
Bradford
MEMORIES

The publishers would like to thank the following companies for their

support in the production of this book

Main Sponsor
Hart & Clough Print Group

Bombay Stores
Bradford & Bingley plc
Bradford College
Bradford Grammar School
Bradford Markets
Bulmer & Lumb Group
G W Butler Ltd
CarnaudMetalBox Engineering
Christeyns UK
Dickinson Caravans
Field Packaging
Gill Demolitions Ltd
The Girls' Grammar School, Bradford
HC Slingsby plc
Joseph A Hey
Holmes, Mann & Co. Ltd
Trevor Iles Limited
Kirgate Shopping Centre
Henry Lewis & Son Ltd
Sydney Packett & Sons Ltd
Provident Financial plc
SLI Lighting plc
Stylo
Whaleys (Bradford) Ltd
Whitaker & Co. (Denholme) Ltd
Don Whitley Scientific Limited
H S Wood
Uriah Woodhead & Son Ltd
Yorkshire Building Society

First published in Great Britain by True North Books Limited
England HX3 6AE
01422 344344

ISBN 1 903204 92 5

Text, design and origination by True North Books
Printed and bound by Hart & Clough Print Group

MORE
Bradford
MEMORIES

CONTENTS

INTRODUCTION

'**M**ore Bradford Memories' is the latest in the series of nostalgia publications from True North, the company that excels in bringing you a view of life as it was in the last century. The book complements previous ones under the 'Memories' banner and takes the reader even further into the very essence of the developing 20th century that shaped our city and made it one of the nation's most illustrious metropolises. It is one of the most comprehensive books the company has yet produced, offering hundreds of images, captions and studies of commercial and private enterprise that go hand in glove with day to day life on the streets.

The city name is derived from the broad ford at Church Bank, below the site of the cathedral, around which a settlement developed during Saxon times. A small town became centred upon Kirkgate, Westgate and Ivegate, but it was razed by the Normans in 1070 after an unsuccessful uprising against William I whose forces had defeated Harold's army at the Battle of Hastings four years earlier. Even the Domesday Book referred to the district as being 'like a waste'. What is now one of Britain's largest cities, Bradford grew at a snail's pace during the Middle Ages, though the right to hold a market was granted in 1147. The Manor of Bradford was under the control of the De Lacy family until 1311, to whom a further market charter was granted by Henry III in 1251. It was not long after this that the first mention of a wool weaver was recorded, an industry, of course, that would become hugely important in Bradford's development many centuries hence. Looking around the area today, it is hard to visualise that the population back then was measured in hundreds. An estimate of just 650 residents was made in the year that the control of the manor passed from the De Lacys to the Earl of Lincoln. Later that century, an influx of Flemish weavers, dyers and fullers into the country had an influence on the cottage industry that was still just a burgeoning trade in the Bradford area. However, the Black Death hit the area and any growth in population was reversed by its devastating effect and the number of local inhabitants was reduced to just 325. However, Bradford recovered and by the late 15th century was, along with Halifax, Ripon, Almondbury, Leeds and Pontefract, one of the main woollen centres in the north of England.

Bradford continued to grow slowly and, by 1620, the manor had passed into private hands. During the English Civil War the town was Parliamentarian in sympathy, but changed hands several times as it was difficult to defend and was besieged in 1642 and again the following year. These unsettled times meant a decline in the town's fortunes, but better days lay ahead and, with greater stability in the late 17th and early 18th centuries,

Bradford's woollen industry began to grow in importance. The addition of turnpikes and canal links encouraged trade to develop as the birth of the industrial revolution was ushered in. By the late 1700s, Bradford was a thriving town of 16,000 souls. Much of the spinning and weaving took place in local cottages and farmsteads, but all that was about to change. Bradford was connected to the Leeds-Liverpool Canal in 1774 and this encouraged the building of woollen mills. By the end of the 18th century, six had been built in the town. The development of worsted manufacture increased this number and by 1810 Bradford was responsible for a quarter of the West Riding's production of worsted. It was not for nothing that it was nicknamed 'Worstedopolis'. Yorkshire boasted plentiful supplies of iron ore, coal and soft water which were used in cleaning raw wool. A huge coal seam provided the power that the industry needed. Sandstone, Bradford's local stone, was an excellent resource for the building of the mills and the large population of West Yorkshire meant there was a readily available workforce. By the 1850s, Bradford had become the wool capital of the world with a population of 100,000, leading to the development of a solid engineering and manufacturing base and a key financial centre which has continued to flourish ever since. The growth was also helped by the opening of the Leeds and Bradford Railway in 1846. A large number of Irish immigrants found work in the town and the 1861 census shows that only just over a quarter of the inhabitants had been born locally.

One of the most important figures in this period was born in 1815. Samuel Lister set up business with his brother John as worsted spinners and manufacturers in Manningham Mills, later to become known as Lister's Mill. He invented the Nip Comb, a device that separated and straightened raw wool, and helped revolutionise the industry and turn himself into a multi-millionaire, as well as being the provider of thousands of jobs in the town. However, not all was rosy in the textile business. The introduction of the steam engine to drive machinery increased the number of mills. With over 200 factory chimneys continually churning out black, sulphurous smoke, Bradford gained the reputation of being the most polluted town in England. There were regular outbreaks of cholera and typhoid and only a third of children born to textile workers reached the age of fifteen. Life expectancy, of just over eighteen years, was one of the lowest in the country. Another famous Bradford name decided to act. Titus Salt, who owned five textile mills in Bradford, was one of the few employers in the town who showed any concern for this problem. After much experimentation, Salt discovered that the Rodda Smoke Burner produced very little pollution and in 1842 arranged for these burners to be used in all his factories. He became the mayor in 1848 and tried to get other mill owners to use the burners, but with little success. Being a man of principle, Salt decided to move his industry out of Bradford and relocated near Shipley in the 1850s. He founded Saltaire, building 850 houses for his workers. It also had its own park, church, school, hospital, library and a whole range of different shops. The houses were far superior to those available in other industrial towns, having piped fresh water, gas and their own outside toilets. He

died in 1876, having spent most of his wealth on good causes. Bradford became a city in 1897, not long before the first of the vast majority of the photographs in 'More Bradford Memories' were taken. Having considered some of the periods that helped forge the modern city, it is now time to concentrate on the years through which our parents and grandparents lived. Already many of us have forgotten or never fully experienced life as it was before the onset of ring roads, flyovers and underpasses. There really was an age, not too long ago, when the car did not reign supreme and when children played with homemade toys. People went shopping in the market for fresh produce and families sat round tables together to eat meals. They listened to the radio, grouped in front of a crackling set that brought 'Dick Barton', 'ITMA' and Henry Hall's orchestra into the front room. Out on the streets rag and bone men called out for business, offering to exchange unwanted household scrap for pegs to be used on the washing line and donkey stones to enhance the appearance of the doorstep. Within the pages of this book the reader will be able to return to those days when our monarchs were revered and our newsreels were full of British achievement. Bradford has much to be proud of and a number of its best known and longest established firms have allowed us to access their internal archives. This has enabled us to recount the history of these companies from humble beginnings, in most cases, to leading positions in their chosen area of expertise. These organisations have tremendous social, as well as commercial significance, as between them they represent the places of employment for many thousands of Bradford people. We are very grateful to the directors of these businesses for their co-operation and valuable support. Let the nostalgia begin.

Left: With all the remodelling that took place in the second half of the last century, it is difficult to get one's bearings when looking towards the city centre as it was in the 1940s. A couple of obvious landmarks can help as we have, on the right, the war memorial that stands in front of the statue of Queen Victoria and City Hall in the distance, with Town Hall Square or Centenary Square, as it became in 1997. That was the year in which we celebrated the anniversary of our city status, an honour granted by Queen Victoria to mark her own diamond jubilee. Our war memorial, sculpted by city architect Walter Williamson, was unveiled on 1 July 1922 in memory of those who fell in World War I. Stone from Bolton Woods Quarry was used and the monument is flanked by realistic figures of a soldier and sailor. Sadly, their original bayonets are now missing as a mixture of vandalism and pacifism in the 1960s determined that they were surplus to requirements. The date of the unveiling held a poignancy that few could fail to notice. It took place on the sixth anniversary of the start of the Battle of the Somme, the conflict in which so many locals, including those from the Bradford Pals, laid down their lives. The roll of honour contains 37,000 names, about as many as in the crowd that attended the unveiling.

STREET SCENES

Forster Square has now gone for good, or at least in a form that anyone will be able to remember without the aid of photographs. So quickly do our own memories fade as we looked across the area that became a development site in the first decade of this century. In years to come we might forget that there was anything else here other than the Broadway Shopping Centre and city centre apartments. Once upon a time, the square and gardens were packed with people and vehicles going about their daily business. This scene from the 1920s was repeated, with differing styles of transport and personal fashion, for the rest of the century and into the new millennium. Poor old William Forster, as even he had to come down from his plinth as the statue was taken away for safe keeping. What would he have thought of all the change? Forster was one of the prime movers of the 1870 Education Act when, as MP for Bradford, he helped lay down the foundations for a national school system.

Below: St Peter's House, formerly the Central Post Office, has somehow managed to survive everything from the Luftwaffe to the even greater damage done to our heritage by architects and planners. It still stands today, though everything else around it, with the exception of the cathedral, has disappeared. Forster Square as we knew it, even before the monstrous Forster House was built, is no more. It exists purely in photographs and in our memories. St Peter's House, a Grade II listed building designed by Henry Tanner, after closing as a post office was used in more recent times by the Life Force Faith Museum, before being taken over by the Millennium Commission and sold on to the Kala Sangam, a South Asia arts group. Three quarters of a century ago it was our main post office and had already clocked up nearly 50 years' service when this view was captured. The No 26 tram to Baildon Bridge operated until 1936. It was then replaced by the red and cream livery of the West Yorkshire Road Car Company's buses. The advert for Swan Vestas, 'the smoker's match, on the front of the tram at least provides us with one of few other constants we can take from the photograph. Made by Bryant and May, they lit their first pipe in July 1861.

Above: It was market day and both shoppers and stallholders had parked up ready for a busy day as a solitary horse and cart made its way along Broadway. Bradford received its first market charter in 1251 and a remnant of the old market cross is retained in the present Kirkgate Market that replaced the Victorian one of the same name. William Morrison was one of the most famous of the stallholders from that era. He started selling butter and eggs there in 1899 and laid the foundation for the Morrison's supermarket chain that opened its first self service store in 1958. The modern Kirkgate Market opened in 1973, but older shoppers still miss the surroundings of the imposing building that was built in 1878 as a replacement of an earlier market. Here, shoppers walked beneath a cast iron frame that contained two 60 foot-high domes and under the huge figures of Pomona and Flora who stood over the arched entrance. It oozed class instead of convenience.

Left: Founded in 1888, H Dawson Sons and Company now has its headquarters at Essex Street, near Bowling back Lane. Harry Dawson sailed to Australia in 1887 on a wool purchasing expedition at time when demand for raw materials was high and the sheep population down under was soaring. On his return, he established a business that has now passed through four family generations. On the other side of Hall Ings, the Bradford Dyers' Association building belonged to the organisation that was a combination of Bradford commission dyeing firms, founded in 1898, that became very large and successful as it dominated the industry in the area. It was taken over by the Viyella group in 1964. Further evidence of the importance of the wool trade comes from the story of the Cathedral's gratitude to the commodity during the English Civil War. Bales of wool were hung over the tower to protect it from cannonballs during the sieges of 1642-43. It is said that the city was spared being sacked because of an apparition that the Earl of Newcastle saw during his stay at Bolling Hall. A woman appeared to him as he lay resting in his room one night and wailed 'Pity poor Bradford'. He was so unnerved that he heeded her wishes.

Above: The guns had been silenced and the planes grounded. The dreadful days of the war were now history, but still a painful memory for people going about their business on Sunbridge Road in 1946. There were reminders of those days all around the city when locals went past the ruins of bombed-out buildings or came across bomb sites that waited, in some cases many years, for new life to be injected. Sunbridge Road still has some of the fine Victorian buildings that were built for the commercial world in Gothic and Classical styles. The road was built as a bypass to Ivegate and the town centre and, by 1870, a group of these impressive structures appeared. The Prudential building in the distance stands out as it was the only major one in the town, as it then was, to be built of red brick and terracotta. Designed by Alfred Waterhouse (1830-1905), the architect best remembered for London's Natural History Museum, it opened for business in 1895. Saxone shoe shop, on the left, was based on the ground floor of the Mechanics' Institute, demolished in 1974.

Lingard's department store, Westgate, was just one of the buildings to take a direct hit in August 1940 when the Luftwaffe's bombers dropped their incendiaries and high explosives on the city centre. The store was later rebuilt on the opposite side of the road, on the corner with Godwin Street, though it finally closed in 1977. But, during the blitz on our cities we had no time to think of the distant future. Today and tomorrow were all that counted. The aftermath of the raid meant hard and dangerous work for the fire and ambulance crews. The volunteer civil defence groups of ARP wardens, WVS members and the like were on hand to lend assistance, even though the flames licked around them and falling masonry was a constant danger. In the morning, council workmen began the tidying up process. Westgate was cordoned off and scaffolding erected around the gutted Lingard's. The British Shoe Company was also badly damaged, as were many other buildings in the city on the night when 116 bombs rained down.

Above: A huge amount of the nation's housing stock was damaged or destroyed during enemy bombing raids in World War II. There was no opportunity to rebuild as everything was geared up to the war effort. Dilapidated properties due for renewal or replacement in 1939 remained standing, and when hostilities ceased the country was in urgent need of places to house a displaced population. With no time and little money available, it was of paramount importance that, somehow, homes could be provided. The prefabricated dwelling was one quick alternative. First seen in 1944, the prefab was promoted by the then Minister of Works, Wyndham Portal, as the way forward. This estate was erected on Hall Lane, south of the city, and included converted Anderson air raid shelters as an addition to the corrugated homes. The single storey structures were only really meant to accommodate small families and were seen as a temporary measure. Yet, we all know that the word 'temporary' means all things to all men and some people spent many years in such homes before being rehoused. A significant minority, however, enjoyed the compact nature of the prefab and were quite happy to remain there. This estate was demolished in 1960, but there are a few examples of emergency postwar housing still in existence today in isolated pockets across the country.

Right: In 1959, Heppleston's general store stood on the corner of Rawson Square at the top of Darley Lane. The

humble flower seller on the street outside plied her trade under the shadow of the statue to the local humanitarian, Richard Oastler (1781-1861). The son of a linen merchant in Thirsk, he then moved to Leeds and became steward of the Fixby estates in Huddersfield. His statue was originally sited in Forster Square before moving here, but can now be found by the shopping centre named after him. He was something of a mixed bag in his views on the rights of others. He was opposed to Catholic emancipation and women's suffrage, but was a prime mover in the anti-slavery movement that was spearheaded by William Wilberforce. He is best remembered though, as can be seen by the inclusion of two other figures on his memorial, for his work in the 1820s and 1830s when he

toiled at some personal and financial cost in the interests of the plight of children in the workplace. John Wood of Horton Hall, a local manufacturer who had introduced many reforms into his factory, told Oastler of the evils of child labour in the Bradford district and made him promise to work towards removing them. He lobbied strenuously in supporting reforms that brought about the Factory Act and railed against some of the restrictive provisions of the Poor Laws. He devoted so much time and money to the cause that he was reduced to penury and served three years in a debtors' prison as a result.

Below: The van belonging to Luther Wright's Pet Emporium, a company still in business today on Sunbridge Road, was heading along Aldermanbury towards the grand looking New Victoria on Princes Way. This handsome theatre was built on the site of the old William Whittaker Brewery that brewed its last pint there in 1928. The New Victoria was built as a vast auditorium with 3,318 seats on three levels, and opened on Monday, 22 September 1930. Operating as a dual purpose cinema and theatre, the large stage included a moving platform that could transport an entire orchestra from the back of the stage to the front. The orchestra pit included a Wurlitzer pipe organ on a rising platform, a most impressive sight. Built by Bradford's own William Illingworth, it cost a mammoth £250,000 to build and boasted that it used some 2,000,000 bricks and 1,000 tons of steel in its complex construction. The first offering was a mix of film and live performances that included a movie version of the farce 'Rookery Nook' and a futuristic revue, 'Follies of 1980'. The building also housed a fine restaurant and ballroom. From 1950, the latter became known as the Gaumont Ballroom and it was a carefully selected 45, 'Sea of Heartbreak' by American country singer Don Gibson, that was the last record played there when it closed on 30 December 1961. The New Victoria/Gaumont became the Odeon Film Centre in 1969 before closing in 2000.

Below: Like some precursor of a 1960s' television advert for Rael Brook Poplin (the shirt you don't iron), this line of washing hung over the cobbled setts of a Bradford back street in August 1951. Row upon row of terraced housing was typical of the working class areas of the city and still is in many places. However, the 21st century remnants of this form of housing are a far cry from the middle of the last century. Although plumbing had been updated from the days when people used outside toilets in the back yard and scrubbed themselves clean in an old tin bath in front of the fire, there was little in the way of the washday aids that the modern housewife has today. That is, of course, if such a person even exists any more. In those seemingly far off postwar days, the woman of the house was expected to provide the household laundry service, cleaning operations and food preparation. Few people in this environment could afford washing machines, fridges, electric vacuum cleaners or irons. A gas or electric stove was the one luxury that families managed to save up for, but some still cooked on open ranges or heated ovens via a back burner connected to the fireplace. Running a home was a tiring job and a full time one as well.

Right: There was no need for a harness, special boots or safety hat. This lamplighter was perfectly happy to climb his ladder and attend to the street light without the need of such fripperies. Perhaps, though, this chap was an engineer attending to a fault at Cowper Place as a lamplighter usually carried a wick on a long pole to enable him to get the lamp working as dusk arrived. He returned at the break of day, this time with a hook attached to that same pole so that he could extinguish the flame. Generally, he worked from ground level. In this instance, perhaps our man was renewing the mantle. The Scottish author, RL Stevenson, was moved to dedicate a poem to 'Leerie the Lamplighter' when he reminisced about seeing him as he lay on his sick bed as a child. Streetlights have a long history in Britain. The Mayor of London, as far back as 1417, instructed householders to hang out lanterns at night during the winter months. Various fuels, such as beeswax or the oil from whales, fishes, sesame seeds and nuts, were used. The introduction of gaslight on our streets in the early 19th century not only improved visibility but also helped reduce crime. This form of illumination gave way to low-pressure sodium and high-pressure mercury lighting in the 1930s, though many of the old standards and cases were retained for a while and have become collectable items in recent times.

Below: This photograph is undated and untitled, but it is amusing for the angle at which it was taken. It purports to suggest that the striped barber's pole was as high as the surrounding chimney pots, but it is just a neat bit of trick photography. The pole itself has its own history. The red and white stripes are a link with the medieval practice of bloodletting as a curative. In those times, barbers doubled as surgeons, though some might think that a butcher would have been a more appropriate choice for that form of alternative medicine. The original pole had a brass basin at the top that represented the vessel in which leeches were kept and one at the bottom that suggested the receptacle in which blood was collected. The pole itself stood for the staff that the patient gripped as he underwent the painful process. Before the days of unisex salons and hairdressing parlours, the barber was a busy man, doling out short back and sides to each and every customer, along with a close shave from the sharp, cut-throat razor that was kept in pristine condition by use of the leather strop. Sixty years ago we slapped on Brylcreem to look as handsome as Denis Compton and nodded discreetly when asked if we needed anything for the weekend.

Below: In February 1964, the Victoria Buildings held a variety of retail outlets. The prominent sign for Fred Truelove, turf accountant, is truly a period piece. The job description was an attempt to show that this was a reputable profession as betting history was littered with examples of dirty dealing and corruption. There is a long history of betting in this country. It became particularly popular during the reign of Charles II, a king who was known to favour horseracing. Titled English gentlemen could be found striking wagers with each other on Newmarket Heath and gradually bookmakers came into being, ensuring a market for those who wished to back their fancies. During this period, bookmaking was conducted by various individuals and regulation as wc know it did not exist. Correspondingly, it was subject to much abuse. As time went by and the working classes became involved in enjoying a flutter and with street betting being illegal, cash bets were placed with bookies' runners who took the money and written record of the wagers to their bosses. In 1961 cash betting shops were legalised and regulated.

Above: Broadway House is the dominant feature of this city centre view, taken in March 1967. Over 40 years later the development for the Broadway Shopping Centre is the less attractive focal point nearby. The early plans to alter the face of our city had already been put into place when this photograph was taken and soon parts of it would be unrecognisable. Word on the streets was about the creation of new roads and the scrapping of some fine, historic buildings. Those discussing events further afield would have been interested in the plight of the stricken oil tanker, the Torrey Canyon. Television audiences were gripped by the newsreel footage of RAF fighter planes strafing the sinking ship in an effort to burn the oil that gushed forth and fouled Cornish beaches.

Above: Tyrrel Street at its junction with Thornton Road was photographed on a bright and sunny day in the early 1970s. The advert for Wills' Capstan cigarettes is a reminder of those days when many of us used to take a drag on a full strength one before breakfast and then have to sit down until the dizzy spell had passed! Although the snapshot is not dated more accurately, it must be right at the beginning of the decade as trolley buses did not run in the city after early 1972. The mother with the three children starting to cross the road near the Belisha beacon, could well have been one of the first of the baby boomers born just after the second world war. This generation changed many of the morals of British society that the old guard took for granted. During the 'swinging-60s' they developed their own culture and redefined some of the traditional standards.

Below left: The Alhambra Theatre still flourishes on what is now Prince's Way and the New Victoria/Odeon building can be seen on its corner of Thornton Road, running to its right here, but the latter building has long been derelict. Tyrell Street, though, seen on 18 March 1965 is largely no more. Only a remnant of it, on the far side of Centenary Square, has survived the bulldozers that changed the face of this section of Bradford beyond recognition in the final quarter of the last century. Tyrell Street took its name from the name of a spot where, in much earlier times, youths once favoured as a place in which to congregate and where people enjoyed the dubious pleasures of cockfighting as a relief from the bull baiting on Westgate. Various spellings, such as Turles, Turls, Tyrls and Tyrrles, were used over the years, leading to the current name of this street. Some think that the word originally derived from a Danish one for a rivulet, while others hold to the theory that it meant a clearing of good grass. The Alhambra was built in 1914 by Chadwick and Watson for the impresario Frank Laidler. He was known as 'the pantomime king' and many famous stars have appeared here in major Christmas productions that have had audiences rolling in the aisles. Norman Evans, George Formby, Ken Dodd, Jimmy Wheeler and Freddie Frinton are just a few of those who tickled our ribs.

Below: It may have been the 'swinging-60s', but Wakefield Road was quiet as people went about their business in the library, at the baths or visiting St John's Church. This decade saw great changes in lifestyle as the country emerged from the austere 1950s. Employment was as high as our expectations and there was optimism in the air. Change meant doing away with some of the old and bringing in the new and that was best reflected in the youth culture. Those whose childhood was spent during or immediately after the war years were not content to accept the values to which their parents clung. After all, or so they believed, it was those standards that had lost an empire, dragged us into international conflict and brought us to our economic knees. The younger generation rebelled and demanded a voice. The establishment was its enemy and had to be altered. Young people behaved differently from their parents as the lads grew their hair long and the girls adopted shorter and shorter skirts. Many regarded marriage as an institution that could be delayed or put off completely. Their music was as brash as their attitudes and it was no surprise to see the old school tie of the Tory government replaced by the cloth cap of the Labour Party. Make love not war was the motto for many as they demonstrated against nuclear arms and sought equality in gender and race.

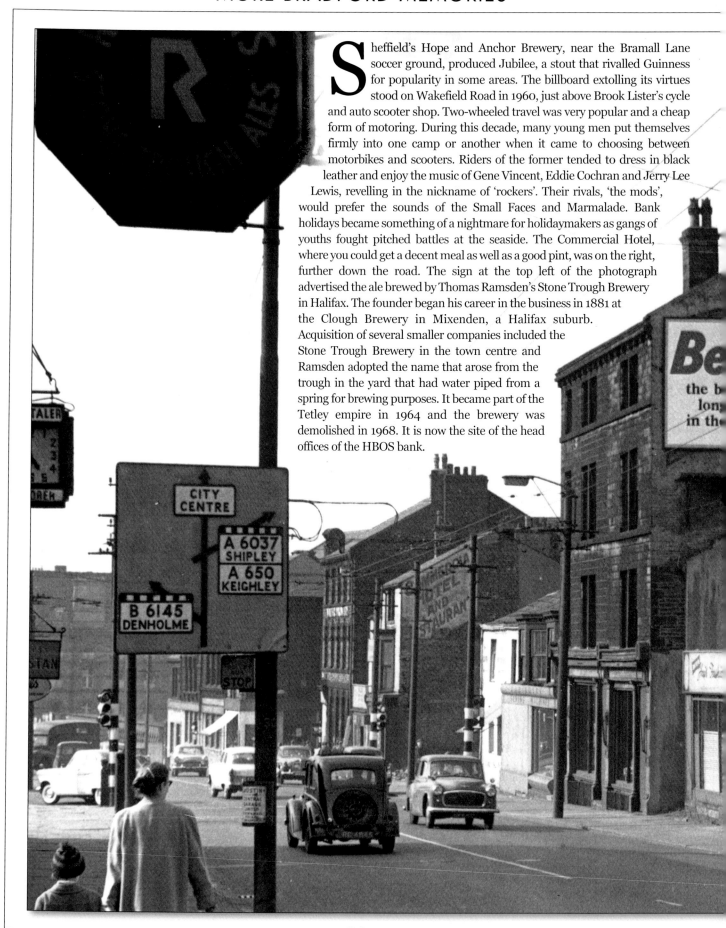

Sheffield's Hope and Anchor Brewery, near the Bramall Lane soccer ground, produced Jubilee, a stout that rivalled Guinness for popularity in some areas. The billboard extolling its virtues stood on Wakefield Road in 1960, just above Brook Lister's cycle and auto scooter shop. Two-wheeled travel was very popular and a cheap form of motoring. During this decade, many young men put themselves firmly into one camp or another when it came to choosing between motorbikes and scooters. Riders of the former tended to dress in black leather and enjoy the music of Gene Vincent, Eddie Cochran and Jerry Lee Lewis, revelling in the nickname of 'rockers'. Their rivals, 'the mods', would prefer the sounds of the Small Faces and Marmalade. Bank holidays became something of a nightmare for holidaymakers as gangs of youths fought pitched battles at the seaside. The Commercial Hotel, where you could get a decent meal as well as a good pint, was on the right, further down the road. The sign at the top left of the photograph advertised the ale brewed by Thomas Ramsden's Stone Trough Brewery in Halifax. The founder began his career in the business in 1881 at the Clough Brewery in Mixenden, a Halifax suburb. Acquisition of several smaller companies included the Stone Trough Brewery in the town centre and Ramsden adopted the name that arose from the trough in the yard that had water piped from a spring for brewing purposes. It became part of the Tetley empire in 1964 and the brewery was demolished in 1968. It is now the site of the head offices of the HBOS bank.

Above: Climbing the hill out of the city centre along Wakefield Road, the line of cars suggested that the motor car was becoming something of a standard item for every family in 1960. No longer was it reserved for the men in suits as the cost of motoring fell in real terms. Higher levels of employment and hire purchase deals meant that the lower classes could indulge themselves in what was rapidly being seen as both a pastime and a necessity. Gone were the days when you saved until you had enough money to buy an item. With a guaranteed pay packet, people were happy to extend themselves and buy 'on tick'. The austere 50s gave way to the swinging 60s and there was a real feel good factor in the air.

Above: During the 1950s there was a boom in private car ownership as the cost of motoring fell in real terms and the country entered a period of economic stability as we emerged from the austerity of the immediate postwar era. Sales of affordable family saloons, like the Ford Prefect and Popular or the Morris Minor and BMC Mini, meant that the man in the street could now become the man behind the wheel. The car was no longer solely the province of the middle classes. Even the prime minister, Harold Macmillan, was moved to say that 'You've never had it so good'. But with the rise in the number of vehicles on the road there came the obvious corollary, the traffic jam. Town centres snarled up and link roads were clogged with bumper to bumper traffic, especially at peak times. When Dr Beeching announced the first of his swingeing cuts to railway services in the early 1960s, further pressure was put on the local and national highways. The first motorways, the M6 and M1, were extended and work on others commenced, including the M62 that eventually connected Liverpool with Hull. The construction of by-passes and ring roads changed forever the face of our urban centres. This scene, taken from Bridge No 1 on Wakefield Road, shows part of the work being done at Dudley Hill on 9 April 1969 as the underpass was developed.

Below: The 1960s and 1970s saw major redevelopment in most of Britain's towns and cities, largely because of the ever increasing demands of the transport system. Here we can see demolition work taking place on 13 September 1975 during the period that saw the end of the old Exchange Station and the creation of the new Interchange that was built and would come to link rail and train services. However, it did not take on its current name until 1983 when it was decided that the title would be appropriate to reflect the nature of the association between public transport on the road and railway. The original railway station was opened by the joint efforts of the Lancashire and Yorkshire Railway and the Great Northern Railway on 9 May 1850, although the station was rebuilt nearer the city centre in 1867, With the rise in popularity of rail travel forcing the companies to expand their operations, the station was completely rebuilt in 1880 with 10 platforms. By the 1970s, the station was deemed too large for the volume of transport using it and the station was closed in 1973 and replaced by the smaller four platform station. The adjoining Bridge Street goods depot was demolished around the same time 1976 and the site was used as a car park. In 2000, the new crown court was built where the original station stood.

AT LEISURE

The city bonfire was part of the celebrations held in Allerton for the coronation of King Edward VII in 1902. It was certainly going to be a magnificent blaze that would light up the night sky for miles around. All manner of flammable materials were piled high in a sight that would give the modern day health and safety executive an apoplectic fit. Fortunately for those who enjoyed fun, such a force of killjoys had not yet been invented. A solitary bobby was quite sufficient to ensure that good sense reigned supreme and he was looking forward to the spectacle just as much as any local. After all, in 1902 you had to be approaching your dotage if you could recall the last time that the nation celebrated the crowning of a new monarch. That had been back in 1838, a year after the death of William IV, when Victoria took the throne. Of those portrayed here, only the bearded gentleman next to the policeman might have had a clear memory of that event. Queen Victoria reigned for nearly 64 years and Edward had to wait until he was 59 before his turn came. That made him the second oldest to accede to the throne, but it is a record that may yet be passed by the current Prince of Wales.

Above: Jerome K Jerome's 'Three men in a boat' described a fanciful river journey by a group of friends on the Thames in Victorian England. Perhaps it inspired this outing on the canal near Bingley that took place in the early years of the last century. The Leeds-Liverpool Canal was not built to provide pleasure trips for the middle classes, but many took the opportunity to enjoy the waters that helped boost Bradford's large woollen industry. The canal was constructed in 1774 so that cloth merchants could gain access to wider markets and more easily transport raw materials. Initially, two main sections were opened, from Liverpool to Wigan and from Leeds to Gargrave. The company ran out of money and the joining of the two parts was not achieved until 1816. Passengers travelled along the canal virtually from its opening. Packet boats worked between Liverpool and Wigan, with the service extended to Manchester after the Leigh branch opened in 1821. They also operated in Yorkshire, but the number of locks here made the service slow. The canal travels through the centre of Bingley and then climbs dramatically up the side of the valley in the famous Bingley Five Rise Locks. It is the steepest flight of locks in the United Kingdom, with a gradient that gives a rise of 59 feet over a distance of 320 feet.

Above right: All the world's a stage and all the men and women merely players. Shakespeare's 'As you like it', though, was not the production being put on at the Princes Theatre in this snapshot, if the scenery and props are a true guide. It was built on what became Victoria Square in 1876, but despite being badly damaged in a fire two years later, emerged as one of Bradford's top venues and was host to many music hall greats, including the Scot, Arthur Lloyd, who impressed audiences with his humorous recitations and fine baritone singing voice. Remodelled by Jackson and Longley in 1900, the Prince's put on popular pantomimes every year that attracted full houses thanks to the appearances of top names such as Florrie Ford and Mona Vivian. The theatre was also the venue for one of the earliest paying film shows that took place in its basement in 1896 when the first demonstration outside London of the Lumiere Cinematograph took place. The building was unique in that it housed two theatres, one above the other. The lower space was occupied from 1871 by the Star Music Hall, later the Palace Theatre. The complex was demolished in 1964 and the National Media Museum was built on the site in 1983 as the National Museum of Photography, Film and Television.

Lane was bounded by the grounds of Horton Old Hall, built in 1675, but the lane continued to be just a route through open fields until the first of a number of villas built by wealthy merchants and mill owners appeared. This road formed a branch of the Leeds and Halifax Turnpike Trust established in 1741 and a toll bar positioned close to Horton House. Between 1890 and 1908 Morley Street was constructed, which contained a tramway leading to the city centre. As the number of mills proliferated, homes were built close by to accommodate all levels of the social classes who relied on them for their livelihood. The homes were of varying sizes, the affluent living in the same area as the workers, with status marked by differing house styles. Rows of larger villa style residences, such as those on Claremont, were sandwiched between the lower middle class housing of Ash Grove and Manville Terrace. Although looking a little different now, the Fox and Pheasant still provides good ale today.

Below: The Fox and Pheasant at 748 Little Horton Lane, under the management of licensee John Benn, is pictured at the start of the 20th century. Much of the area developed in late Victorian times as Bradford's woollen trade developed and workers left the fields to work in the mills. The southwestern end of Little Horton

Below: Their numbers dwindle with every year that passes, but we must always remember those who fought on our behalf. On Remembrance Sunday, we particularly recall those who gave their lives in service of this country in the two world wars that scarred the last century. On 11 November 1971, both young and old gathered by the cenotaph, under the shadow of the Alhambra Theatre. However, it was the theatre of war that brought the crowds out to listen to the prayers and readings and to bow their heads in a thanksgiving service. Perhaps Britain's most famous cenotaph is the one in London that Lutyens designed. Made from Portland stone, it was unveiled in 1920 and the inscription reads simply, 'The Glorious Dead'. Every town and village has its own form of cenotaph and, while the style and size of these memorials vary considerably from place to place, the message is the same all over, 'Lest we forget'. It was on the eleventh hour of the eleventh day of the eleventh month in 1918 that the guns of Europe fell silent as the armistice was signed in a railway carriage in the Forest of Compiegne, France. In 1919, King George V issued a proclamation calling for two minutes' silence at 11 am on the second Sunday in November. Armistice Day was renamed Remembrance Day after the second world war.

Above: By April 1969, the workmen were well under way with diverting the course of Manchester Road from in front of the Odeon westwards towards the Alhambra, leaving the cinema isolated on a large island along with the older properties to the rear. It had already shown its last movie, 'The Thomas Crown Affair', on Saturday, 22 March and the distinctive building soon made way for the new Magistrates' Courts and gardens that would be built on the site. The cinema had, for some 30 years, been one of the main sources of entertainment in the city. The demolition of the former Central Mills Wool Combing Company building provided a large prime site at the bottom of Manchester Road adjacent to the Oddfellows Arms pub that was bought by Oscar Deutsch's Odeon chain. Deutsch saw Bradford as a prosperous city and awash with money through its wool, textile and engineering industries. With so much wealth abounding, he knew that his cinema would attract a large clientele and so he built the largest new cinema of the Odeon Theatre chain. The imposing frontage had a wide entrance of five oak and glass pairs of double doors with a second set of doors inside. To the left of the entrance was a huge tower largely of glass. Somewhat quaintly, despite the example of most other comparable cinemas, an organ was not installed in the Odeon. Few of Deutsch's chain had them as he thought them unnecessary. The cinema opened on 17 December 1938, but only survived in its original form until being bombed in 1940. It was soon rebuilt, but remodelled again in 1961.

Above: The children's pool at Bradford's Lister Park Lido, seen around the late 1940s, was crowded with happy bathers enjoying the northern sunshine. Some of the girls were bareheaded, but many of the others sported a variety of headgear from flowery swimming caps to turbans. The dress sense of these females was a far cry from the stern attitudes displayed by their forebears who took the coastal waters from the privacy of a bathing machine in Victorian times. Even in the early part of the last century, mixed bathing was seen by some as the first step on the road that led down the slippery slope to immorality. That mattered little to these children. Splashing around in the open air was great fun, though the polio scare in the early 1950s meant that for a while such places of entertainment felt the pinch. Parents were worried that their loved ones might contract the contagious and devastating disease via contact in crowded places and attendances at swimming baths and lidos fell for a while.

Below: Ilkley Lido is one of the few open air pools left in Yorkshire, but Bradford once had its very own in Lister Park. During the summer months, especially in the school holidays, its waters were packed with families enjoying the freedom of pretending to be Johnny Weissmuller, Ian Black, Dawn Fraser or Esther Williams. There was a lido in Victorian times, some 400 yards northwest of what is now Cartwright Hall, but it went in 1890. The one that readers might recall was built in 1930 and is seen here in its heyday, just after the last war. The diving boards and slides gave young bucks the chance to show off their devil may care attitude in front of giggling girls who pretended to be impressed. Unfortunately, the cost of the pool's upkeep became too much for the Council to bear. The usual platitudes when making cutbacks were heard, but as usual it was the ordinary folk who suffered when one of their prized amenities was closed in 1973. The Lido was finally demolished in 1991.

Below: Enjoying the sunshine on a Sunday afternoon, the residents of Portland Street, as seen from Manchester Road, sat outside and chatted happily with their neighbours. There was a time when there was a real community spirit on our city streets. Whole families grew up in close proximity to one another and many were born, lived and died on the same street. Grown-up sisters and brothers and grandparents lived just around the corner. Even the people next door were so well known to us that we referred to them as 'auntie' or 'uncle'. If you ran out of sugar on the Sunday, you could always borrow a cupful because the shops were closed until Monday morning. Children played out happily, chalking hopscotch squares on the pavement or cricket stumps on the wall. They stayed out until it got dark without any parental worries. There was little traffic on the side roads in the middle of the last century for us to worry about. Neighbours would also keep a weather eye out for any strangers passing through and we all knew each other's business and were glad to lend a helping hand when times were tough. We donkeystoned the front step, swept the pavement outside the door and gossiped in a friendly fashion about the woman who had just moved into No 23.

Right: Looking from Silk Street, the row of houses belongs to the back of Patent Street. On 29 October 1963, the young man in the foreground owed much of his fashion sense to the late 1950s. His tight trousers, with the straight lines, were similar to the drainpipe style favoured by the Teddy Boys who developed something of a reputation for trouble making, especially on Friday and Saturday nights around town. That is not to say that our featured man belonged to that fraternity, just that he drew on their look. The Edwardian mode of dress, with its long drape jackets, caught on with London youths and soon spread across the country. The Daily Express coined the Teddy Boy title in a headline in 1953 after a series of gang fights. However, as with most other youth cults, most were attracted by the clothes and music rather than violence. By the early 1960s,

the Patent Street district was in need of renewal and its houses stood empty and forlorn. The waste land around attracted fly tippers and abandoned cars provided a dangerous playground for youngsters. Part of Manningham Mills can be seen above the rooftops as Patent Street runs directly adjacent to the long five-storey façade of the warehouse or west wing of the complex and was lined for the rest of its length by a mixture of tall structures that included the boiler house, a warehouse and the 250 foot high campanile chimney.

Below left: Boys will be boys, even when they are in middle age. The real children had to stand and watch with mixed degrees of patience as members of the Bradford Model Engineering Society enjoyed themselves on the miniature railway in Northcliffe Woods, Shipley. Founded in 1908, the society is one of the oldest of its type and the members have other interests as well as locomotives. Some enjoy marine models and others are more interested in road vehicles, but it is the joy of engineering and modelling that unites the. Amos Barber was one of the founder members of the society and many of the models he constructed are exhibited in Bradford's Industrial Museum. He also exhibited one of the traction engines he built on a pioneering television show for the BBC in 1937. In the late 1940s the society's first permanent railway was built at Thackley. It relocated to Shipley in 1966 and, in 1969, a five-inch gauge locomotive 'Pamela' ran for an impressive 60 miles non-stop on a newly constructed track. The marine section of the society now sails on the lake at Bradford Moor Park. Model steam rollers, tractors and other vehicles can often be seen on the woodland paths at Northcliffe.

Hart & Clough - A Name in Large Print

Though Bradford has seen many printing firms come and go down the decades, one firm at least has not only survived but prospered – Hart & Clough Ltd. In the late 19th century George Hart, a compositor with W N Sharpe Ltd, decided to leave his job and go into business on his own account.

On 15th July 1885 he was offered the tenancy of Room 26 at 21 Swaine Street, Bradford at a rent of £17 a year, to be paid quarterly. Two double gas brackets and a gas meter were all the room contained, but George Hart moved in and confidently set up his small printing business.

The choice of premises was a shrewd one: Swaine Street was convenient for the Wool Exchange. From the early 1800s Bradford had been recognised as the centre of the worsted industry and the Wool Exchange, with its hundreds of subscribers, was one of the world's most important markets. With the wool merchants as its main clients, the Hart printing business flourished and three years later he was ready to expand into an adjoining room. On March 15th 1888, for the additional rent of £8 a year - three shillings a week - he took over Room 27 and the small cupboard it contained, though the few alterations that were needed to adapt the room to his purpose cost him an extra 15 shillings. Within days Mr Hart was joined in the business by Ezra Clough. Mr Clough knew the stationery business inside out, having been the manager of a Bradford stationery shop.

The firm became Hart & Clough, Printers, in the mid-1890s.

Ezra Clough was developing a new hobby - photography. The camera had been invented a mere 70 or so years earlier by a French doctor, who in 1826 produced the world's first images from nature on pewter plates with a camera obscura and an eight-hour exposure. The new invention received the royal seal of approval when Queen Victoria posed for her first photograph in 1860. By the end of the century the techniques of photography had progressed in leaps and bounds. In 1889 the Eastman Company produced the Kodak No 1 camera and roll film, giving hand-held snapshots to the world.

In 1897 Ezra Clough proudly recorded images of the machine room and stockroom for posterity. A number of the

fine photographs he took of the Hart & Clough premises in the late 1890s still survive, giving us a rare opportunity to slip back through time and view the old printing presses and equipment, the fixtures and fittings, and the stockroom. It is thanks to Ezra Clough's keen interest in photography that we have these fascinating images of how a small printing business operated in the late 19th century.

Ezra Clough became well known as an amateur photographer, and he eventually became President of the Bradford Photographic Society, a pioneer group of

Left: Ezra Clough. Below: The Machine Room pictured by Ezra Clough in 1897.

A.D. 1886.

BRADFORD OVERSEERS' OFFICE—46, Darley Street.

Mr. George Hart — No. 473

RATEABLE VALUE.		
	£	s.
House - -		
Shop - -		
Office - -	*14*	
Warehouse -		
Mill, &c. -		
Stable -		
Land -		
____Works		
Cottages -		
£		

Township of Bradford—Bradford Union.

The Overseers of the Poor demand payment of the Poor Rate made the **28th day of January, 1886,** and of the Arrears of former Rates as below, now due from you.

Amount of Rate at 3/4 in the pound, on £ ___*14*___ rateable value

Allowance of 25°/₀ to owners of Cottage Property assessed at and below £8.

TOTAL £

£	s.	d.
2	6	8

Particulars of the Rate, or purposes for which the above Rate has been made at 3/4 in the £ respectively— Poor Rate, 8d. ; Borough Rate, including leakage, 2s. 7d. ; other Charges, 1d.

THE ABOVE RATE IS DUE ON DEMAND, and if not then paid, the Overseers request you will pay it at their **OFFICE** within **SEVEN DAYS** from the delivery hereof.

---

enthusiasts which had been founded in 1860. He was the first secretary of the Yorkshire Photographic Union - an association he helped to found in 1899 - and he held the post for an incredible 25 years.

Frank Vincent, Ezra Clough's 16-year-old son, started work at Hart & Clough in August 1907; the young man had no way of knowing, of course, that in joining the firm he had taken the first step towards establishing the business as the traditional family firm that it was eventually to become. Three years later George Hart retired, handing over the business to his partner.

Meanwhile young Vincent, was following in his father's footsteps and developing his own hobbies - though not photography. At the age of 18 he bought his own car and learned not only to drive it but to maintain it - a necessity in those early days of motoring when there were few cars about in Bradford, and even fewer mechanics to mend them when they broke down. Building radio receivers was the young man's other passion. His aim was not to listen to popular music over the airwaves; radio programmes as we know them today were still in their infancy (the world's first radio programme of words and music had only been made four years earlier, in 1906, in the United States). It was in the Morse code messages from ships and from radio hams, the only transmissions at the time, that Vincent's interest lay. Morse code itself is now part of our past, as its use was discontinued in 1999.

BOROUGH OF BRADFORD.

BOROUGH COLLECTOR'S OFFICE, TOWN HALL, BRADFORD

R.O. 18000.—20-2-86

Mr Geo Hart
21 Swaine Street

Dr. To the **BRADFORD CORPORATION.**

FOR RATES AND WATER RENTS, NOW DUE, FOR THE YEAR 1886

This RATE is intended to meet the EXPENSES for GENERAL DISTRICT and WATER PURPOSES, from 1st January, 1886, to 31st December, 1886, (both inclusive)

No. of Assessment.	DESCRIPTION.	RATEABLE VALUE.	GENERAL DISTRICT RATE AT 1/10 IN THE POUND.	WATER RATE AT 2d. IN THE POUND.	WATER RENTS, AS PER SCALE.							TOTAL.
					Amount for Premises.	Bath.	W.C.	Urinal.	Tube.	Horse.	Garge.	
	HOUSE											
	HOUSE AND SHOP											
	SHOP OR OFFICE											
332	WAREHOUSE	14	1 5 8	2 4								1 8
	MILL											

MISCELLANEOUS CHARGES FOR WATER.

ENGINE £ : s. : d. BREWING, &c. £ : s. : d. FIXES £ s. d.

N.B.—This Account being now due, payment to Mr. J. W. GILL, the Borough Collector, is requested, on demand, or at his Office, Town Hall, Bradford.
Office Hours—9 a.m. to 5 p.m. ; on Saturdays from 9 a.m. to 1 p.m.
A separate printed Form of Receipt is specially provided, and no other Receipt will be recognised.

Total....£ 1 8

PROPORTION FROM .... £

As the First World War got into its stride, Hart & Clough acquired W H Butler, a Bradford bookbinding firm, re-launching it as Woods (Bradford) Ltd in 1915. Anxious to fight for his country, Vincent volunteered for military service and in 1916 was commissioned in the West Yorkshire Regiment. Before the war ended, however, he found himself back in Britain, seriously injured by shrapnel - a piece that lodged in his knee was with him until his death. The incident

Top and above: *Rates bills from Bradford Council dated 1886.* ***Right:*** *An early 20th century letterhead.*

could have been far worse, however: Vincent's silver cigarette case, which he carried in his breast pocket, stopped a piece of shrapnel that would otherwise have undoubtedly ended the young man's life prematurely. The cigarette case, complete with a large hole, is still treasured by his family, who value it as a rare piece of family history.

In 1928 a key move was made when Hart & Clough became an incorporated company, with Ezra and Vincent as directors. Ezra died six years later, just one year before his grandson Michael came into the company.

By the mid-1930s, with war once more looming on the horizon, a need for more extensive premises was making itself felt, and the company moved to George Street. Some of the excellent work produced by Hart & Clough at the time has survived, notably a portfolio of elegant sample letterheads. Some of the designs are amazingly intricate, and the quality of the work demonstrates the skills of the engraver and the printer.

When war was declared in 1939 Michael Clough was called up from the Territorial Army - and was closely followed by other members of staff who were of the age for military service. The older members were left to cope as best they could with a smaller workforce and a lack of skilled operatives, yet at the same time dealing with the need for increased production. The firm's van driver became one of those pressed into learning to operate a printing machine!

During the war years one of Hart & Clough's main clients was AV Roe & Co, which built its Avro Lancaster bombers at its factory near Yeadon airport. When the war was over it paid tribute to the work of Hart & Clough, recognising it as the printers who could always be depended on to deal with a rush job. 'Send it to Hart & Clough,' was the usual response to pressure of work - 'They'll get it through in time.' With the return of its staff from the services, Hart & Clough made a significant investment in new printing equipment, and also made another move, this time into Summerville Road. The late 1940s and early 50s were a time of steady growth and change of emphasis within the company, from stationery production to brochures and publicity leaflets.

Those years also brought significant changes in technology within the printing industry, and by 1952 Hart & Clough, determined to remain at the forefront, had installed its first lithographic offset press. It was to be the first of many.

Peter Clough established the fourth generation of the family firm when he joined Hart & Clough in 1965 after graduating from the Printing College in Leeds. His first responsibility was to set up a camera and platemaking department. In 1969 the company's first Solna SRA2 litho machine was purchased, followed by another similar machine a couple of years later. The investment in litho presses led eventually to an expansion in the camera, film-planning and platemaking departments.

New offices and a warehouse were added in 1980, the warehouse being built, owing to the soft nature of the land, on a 'raft' of steel reinforced concrete. Almost 2,000 square feet of floor space was needed for the building, and more than 150 tons of concrete and steel reinforcement were used.

Simultaneously other important renovations were made to the existing building in preparation for the installation of a four-colour Heidelberg GTO press. The new developments made it possible for the company to produce high quality colour printing at a very high speed.

The company made further advances in 1989, when it acquired The Amadeus Press Ltd, a specialist book and magazine printer based in Huddersfield. The Amadeus Press had been established in 1988 by Richard Wadsworth and Richard Cook, following the demise of the long-established Huddersfield book printer Netherwood Dalton. It specialised in transport and local history books, and magazines, printing on large format machines taking a sheet size of 1000 x 1400 mm.

This purchase proved to be a key move, establishing Hart & Clough as one of the leaders in short-run high quality book work. Today any print job can be taken on, from letterheads and business cards to packaging and full-colour books.
In fact, the printing of this very book was undertaken by The Amadeus Press.

Computerisation was a necessary move within a company that was determined to keep abreast of modern technology: computers were brought into the everyday administration of Hart & Clough in the early 1980s. Some of the first software to be installed was an estimating programme developed and written by Michael Clough. In 1991 further developments were made with the introduction of the first computer-controlled four-colour press; a PC network was developed two years later for running the company's management information system (MIS). Richard Clough - the fifth generation of the family, and today's Managing Director - joined the company after graduating from the Manchester University Printing Course in 1993, making the completion of the computer network his responsibility. The introduction of an Apple Mac brought computerisation to yet another area of the factory, enabling designs and artwork for all items of printed matter to be created on screen. Well before the possibility of being overtaken by the 'Millennium bug', a completely new computer network and MIS system was installed in January 1999, ensuring even more streamlined processing of information within the company.

By now however the Summerville Road site was overcrowded, whilst the lease on the Amadeus building in Huddersfield was nearing its end. In November 1999 a 23,000 square foot building at Chain Bar at Junction 26 on the M62 was bought, into which both company operations were moved in April 2000. The building was named Ezra House.

The new building allowed expansion for the pre-press area. A complete new Apple Mac studio was installed and a graphic designer employed for the first time. In 2004 a B1 size five-colour Roland press was acquired to fill the gap between the smaller machines brought from the Bradford site and the large-format machines used to produce the Amadeus books and magazines. To gain further versatility a

B1 size Sanwa die-cutting machine was purchased to cut folders and boxes to shape.

To speed up the plate-making process the next year a Luscher platesetter was installed. The machine images printing plates directly from computers in the design studio, cutting out all film production and handwork involved in film assembly. With the presses moving onto a double day shift system work could now be produced even faster.

Meanwhile Woods (Bradford) Ltd had been operating as a trade finisher for over 90 years, folding, wire-stitching, sewing and perfect binding printed sheets for many local printers not just Hart & Clough. In 2006 it was decided to bring Woods under the same roof as Hart & Clough and Amadeus, so creating a self-contained integrated unit producing all aspects of print work from design through to bound books.

Over the years the company has established a solid philosophy of close involvement with clients while at the same time producing a first class job at a reasonable price.

Since the 19th century the printing industry has developed remarkably. Hart & Clough Ltd in particular has seen changes that its founders could never have imagined. The company's business philosophy of offering a high quality personal service however is one thing that has never changed - and it is Hart & Clough's aim to ensure that this fundamental principle will remain unaltered in the 21st century.

Left: A letter from AV Roe & Co. Ltd expressing its appreciation for the support and effort received from Hart & Clough during the war years. ***Above:*** Hart & Clough's Summerville Road premises in the late 1980s. ***Below:*** Ezra House, Cleckheaton, home to Hart & Clough from 2000.

EVENTS & OCCASIONS

This old photograph of Towngate in Baildon shows the old market cross and stocks to the right. The drinking fountain with its polished granite upper part, behind the bus crew, was manufactured by the monumental masons Beanlands of Little Horton Lane. The Victorian fountain was commissioned by Baron RP Amphlett in memory of his mother-in-law, Mrs Ferrand, who came from St Ives,

Bingley. A street in that town is also named for her family. The village of Baildon has a long history and was recorded by name as long ago as AD 835. However, situated on the edge of a bleak moor it remained an isolated farming community until the transition into an industrial village around the end of the 18th century. After the construction of the railway in the late 19th century, Baildon became a desirable retreat for Bradford's wealthier citizens who enjoyed its relatively unpolluted air and dramatic scenery. Occasionally, travellers camped on the edge of the moor, reviving memories of the days when gypsies held regular carnivals each June in the Jenny Lane area that is now Laburnum Drive. Quite often the occasion would be used to hold wedding celebrations, but during the early 20th century the gatherings became more intermittent before dying out completely at the start of the second world war.

Below: Many members of the royal family have visited Bradford on official visits over the years. Around 1930 The Prince of Wales, the future Edward VIII, inspected the ranks of World War I army veterans, all of whom displayed their campaign medals with a fierce pride. Many remembered that war as one where they served nobly, but one that held much sorrow and pain. The West Yorkshire Regiment (Prince of Wales' Own) was raised in 1685 and soon saw service in Flanders, a mild foretaste of what was to come over 200 years later. In 1876, the Prince of Wales, later Edward VII, presented new colours to the 1st Battalion at Lucknow and conferred on the regiment the title 'The Prince of Wales' Own'. During the 1914-18 war many young men joined up in groups from neighbouring streets and from common professions. They were nicknamed 'Pals' Regiments' and the Bradford Pals were among the most famous because of the carnage that was to decimate them. Officially the 16th and 18th Battalions West Yorkshire Regiment, both part of 93rd Brigade, 31st Division, they arrived on the Somme in early 1916 and took part in the fighting for Serre on 1 July. On that dreadful day the 16th lost 515 officers and men, while the 18th suffered 490 fatalities. No wonder these survivors from the Great War still looked sombre some 15 years later.

Right: On 4 May 1904, Victoria Square was heaving with people craning their necks to see the Prince of Wales, the future King George V. He had arrived in Bradford to perform the ceremonial unveiling of the magnificent statue that had been erected in honour of his grandmother, the late Queen Victoria who had died three years earlier. From the headgear of those in the crowd it is easy to pick out the dignitaries from the hoi polloi. Just look at the top hats on the heads of those who had the equivalent of ringside seats. It took three tons of bronze to cast Alfred Drury's twelve foot high statue that shows the queen as she looked at her golden jubilee in 1887. The flanking lions were sculpted by Alfred Broadbent, a Shipley man. JW Simpson, the person responsible for the building of the first Wembley Stadium and our own Cartwright Hall, designed the pedestal and balustrade. Many of our country's finest statues relate to Victorian figures or were built in that century to honour those who helped put the Great into Britain. Queen Victoria was the monarch who signed a Charter of Incorporation that united the townships of Bradford, Manningham, Bowling and Horton as a borough and, in 1897, put her signature to the document that awarded us city status.

Below: Ernest W Busby, the founder of the Manningham department store, performed the ceremony of laying the foundation stone to the Coronation Extensions, so named because this was the year in which George VI was enthroned at Westminster Abbey. Busby's dominated the city end of Manningham Lane and middle class ladies flocked there, leaving their chauffeurs to wait in their limousines to help with the parcels and hat boxes. Busby was a religious soul, hence the inscription 'Be mindful of the rock of thy strength' on the stone. The photograph was taken on 24 May, 1937 and this coincided with Empire Day. This was often a time for celebration when the country held events that acknowledged Britain's role as a major player on the world stage. Any globe would show huge chunks that were coloured red to show that these countries and territories acknowledged our monarchy as their head of state. That would not last for too much longer. There were already rumblings from that jewel in the crown, India. There, Mahatma Ghandi led nationwide campaigns for the alleviation of poverty, the liberation of women and for brotherhood amongst differing religions and ethnicities. He had one other major aim for his nation, independence. This was achieved in 1947 and other countries in Asia and Africa followed suit over the next two decades.

Right: The size of the large motorcade in Manningham tells us that an important personage was on his way into Bradford. They did not get much more important than King George VI and Queen Elizabeth. On 20 October 1937, the royal couple was part way though a tour of the county and huge crowds flocked to see them everywhere they went. There was no real television at the time and the only footage of such personalities was restricted to the cinema newsreels. Today, we see film and live coverage of celebrities and VIPs so often that we have become blasé about it. But, 70 years ago, such a visit was a chance to see our lords and masters in the flesh. The country was almost exclusively supportive of the monarchy as an institution and whenever any of its members came to see us we got out our Union flags and waved them furiously. Children were given time off school to pay their respects and demonstrate their support. This was a particularly important time for the nation as it was only a few months before that the King had been crowned as successor to his brother, Edward VIII, who had abdicated at the end of the previous year. There were also the storm clouds of war blowing across Europe and it was necessary to show our national solidarity.

Below: Since Brown, Muff and Company ceased trading from this corner of Ivegate and Market Street, various names have been seen above the door. By 2007, the latest, Dillon's Bookstore, had also moved on. The original department store was established in one section of the building here in 1870, with gradual acquisition of neighbouring properties over the years until the whole block belonged to the company by 1934. Three years later, it was time to celebrate the coronation of George VI. His brother, the former Edward VIII, abdicated in December 1936 leaving 'Bertie', as his family knew him, the momentous burden of acceding to the throne whilst being thoroughly unprepared for the role. He opted to use the date already set aside for his brother's coronation, so on 12 May 1937 flags, banners and bunting flew merrily across the street and from poles erected in honour of the important day.

Right: When the Duke of Edinburgh came to call in January 1949, he took time out from his official duties in opening the new Bradford Grammar School to visit Lister Park. Thousands lined the route and spilled across Manningham Lane to catch a glimpse, probably for the first time, of the man who had married the heir to the throne just over a year previously. Princess Elizabeth stayed at home as she had not long given birth to the couple's first child, Charles, but locals were just as happy to see one royal representative as any other. The motorcade made its way through the Norman Arch and into the park that was named for the great industrialist, Samuel Lister. His family already owned land in the area, but the wealth that he accumulated from the textile trade enabled him to develop Manningham Hall and its

estate. He sold it to the Corporation in 1870 for a knock down price with the proviso that it was to be used as a public park. Cartwright Hall, named for the man who invented the power loom, was built around the turn into the 20th century and now serves as a principal art gallery. Locals have enjoyed the grounds for over a century, with the exception of the early 1940s when they were put to agricultural use to support the war effort.

Above right: At the start of the 1930s, Edward, Prince of Wales (1894-1972) was on one of many visits he would make to Bradford and other British towns and cities during the first half of that decade. He was born in Richmond, Surrey, the eldest child of the Duke of York, the future George V, and was known to his family as David, one of his middle names. He was to become the catalyst for one of the largest crises to have hit the monarchy since the days of civil war, invasions and uprisings by followers of pretenders to the throne. As heir to the throne since his mid teens, Edward presented a curious mix of careless immorality and attention to duty during his father's reign. He volunteered to serve at the front during the first world war, but was refused permission because of the value he

might have had to the enemy if captured. He represented the king on various overseas visits in the 1920s, but started to earn himself an unwholesome reputation. This visit to Bradford was one of many he made as part of the royal family's attempt to improve his standing by arranging more home-based tours where he could be in touch with the general public and show concern for the underprivileged in deprived areas. In the end, his own self interest cost him the throne after he refused to give up his lover and later wife, Wallis Simpson.

TRANSPORT

This was one of the first trolleybuses ever seen in Britain and it attracted an interested group of onlookers of all ages at Hodgson Square, Laisterdyke before setting off to Dudley Hill. The No 240 was also known to some as a trackless car, to differentiate it from the tramcars of the period. It must have been a truly magnificent spectacle as it had only been a decade or so earlier that the horse reigned supreme as the power source for most forms of road transport. It was on this route that Bradford's trolleybus service first ran on 20 June 1911. How different the world was in those days. Private cars were in their infancy, there were few electrical appliances, no national radio or television to entertain us and only the occasional biplane in the sky. Supermarkets were several generations away and families tended to stay together. But it was not all sweetness and light as the medical advances that brought us penicillin, advanced vaccines, free education for all and cleaner air and homes were still on the horizon.

Above: Bradford firefighters moved into their state of the art new community fire station on 15 January 2007. The £4 million complex replaced the old Central Fire Station on Nelson Street, seen here in the early 1950s. This building was ahead of its time when it opened on 28 October 1902, so much so that the Lord Mayor, WC Lupton commented that it was the most modern and up to date one in the whole of the United Kingdom. The official ceremony was marked by displays from the brigade crews, followed by a splendid lunch for those who loved organising rather than doing, down at the Town Hall. The building cost £16,000 and contained extensive stabling for the horses that pulled the appliances. It would be several years before the first motorised fire engines came into being. The fire station had an 84 foot long engine house with six bays. There was a 100 yard long drill house and top notch facilities for the crews, including a billiard room and a gymnasium. A new building was erected on the same site and opened in October 1969.

Right: It was a dank day on Main Street, Bingley in 1925. Although we might think that the bumper to bumper traffic is a modern phenomenon, it was generally a busy spot, even early in the last century, despite the evidence of this photograph. In 1904, the road was straightened and the new route cut through an old graveyard that contained the remains of the poet John Nicholson. The Market Hall and stocks once stood on Main Street opposite Ferrand Lane. The tram might have brought ladies into town to take tea at the Loft Café where they could discuss the problems of the world that were tipping us towards anarchy. We had won the Great War, but the country fit for heroes that Lloyd George promised had never materialised. The General Strike was but 12 months away. Bingley had flourished as a town during the 19th century. Following the mechanisation of the worsted industry, mills and houses had invaded the slopes, mainly in the northern side of the ancient township, but, thankfully, failed to destroy completely the beauty of the surrounding dale or the upland neighbouring villages. People migrated from the rural areas to work in the mills, with many coming from further afield, particularly after the Irish potato famine in the 1840s.

wonderful view of the rolling countryside, they were obviously draughty affairs for those hardy souls who perched themselves on the top deck. Rain, an unfortunately frequent visitor to the West Riding, soon drove the passengers inside and the closed top variety of transport was soon the only form of tramcar to be seen as public opinion had its way. Electrically powered trams were first successfully tested in service in America's Richmond, Virginia in 1888. There had been earlier commercial installations of electric streetcars, including one in Berlin, as early as 1881 and another one in Saint Petersburg, Russia the year before. The earlier installations, however, proved difficult or unreliable. The German line, for example, provided power through a live rail and a return rail, akin to the workings of a model train setup. This limited the voltage that could be used and provided unwary people and animals crossing the tracks with a literally hair raising experience! The collection of current from an overhead wire provided the solution and tram travel took off across the world. It even inspired Judy Garland into song about them in her movie 'Meet me in St Louis' when she sang 'Clang, clang, clang went the trolley' in 'The Trolley Song'.

Above: Seen bowling along St Enoch's Road, near Little Horton, the No 138 tram to Wibsey was one of the open topped variety that ran this route in 1908. Although affording a

Left: Roll up, roll up. It was sale time at Busby's and shoppers eager for a bargain came along in large numbers to the Manningham Lane department store. Summer and winter sales were special times when slow moving goods could be disposed of by the retailer at a price that was attractive to the consumer. These were augmented by special lines that were brought in just for the sales' market, though many shoppers did not realise this. The seasonal sale was part of the natural cycle of shopping and was far different from the way that one is conducted now by any large warehouse style outlet of modern times. It invariably appears to be ending next Sunday, only for yet another to start again the week after with the same sort of closing date. The No 24 tram heading towards the camera advertising Buchanan's Black and White whisky was headed for Crossflatts. To its left, a pair of very elegant women, looking most attractive in their figure-hugging dresses, gazed across at the store. Perhaps they had just visited the nearby hairdresser who was offering a permanent wave, as if they needed an enhancement to their already stylish look.

Above: Some things never change. We may not have trolley buses any more, nor is the blue and ivory livery a common sight on our streets, but the queue of people waiting to board a stationary public service vehicle is still with us, as is the attitude of some drivers. Never mind the weather, never mind the ages of the potential passengers, if the bus is not due to admit its customers for another two minutes then they can just lump it, hard to comprehend when you consider in the late 1930s each bus had a conductor as well as a driver. Regardless of this he did not start collecting fares until the journey got under way. This trolley was bound for Clayton. In the background we can see the Town Hall and the end of Thornton Road. An inspector, perhaps the forerunner of Blakey from ITV's 'On the buses', stands guard over the entrance with a 'they shall not pass' stance as the driver and conductor idly chat, oblivious to the frown of disapproval aimed at them by the woman behind the pole.

Below: Looking across Forster Square from the cathedral steps on 18 July 1959, the No 24 trolley bus to Crossflatts was just one of several to be seen in this picture. Bradford's place in trolley bus history is quite significant. Trolley buses were introduced here in 1911 after Parliament approved a bill allowing Bradford Corporation to operate them. Unfortunately, this was not the first such service in the country as Leeds pipped us to the post by just four days. The original idea was for a 'trackless tram' to save the cost of laying track, but having the advantages of electric traction. After various methods of current collection, the twin trolley boom and twin overhead wire system became the norm. Initially, the buses looked more like the trams that they were to replace, but soon took on a more distinctive identity of their own. By 1930, the trolley bus was a clean, swift and very modern looking vehicle. However, so smoothly did they run that some people referred to them as the 'whispering death' as they caught pedestrians crossing the street unawares. With the hilly nature of Bradford's geography, they could deal with the inclines better than most diesel powered buses. However, the cost of upkeeping the overhead wring system, allied to cheaper oil costs at the time, helped to conspire against the continuation of this popular form of public transport. The last services ran on 26 March 1972 and were then replaced by Leyland Atlantean motor buses.

The Cullingworth bus waited outside the gates of the secondary modern school on Bradford Road at Bingley at a time in the 1960s when we still had the national 11-plus examination. Mainly dependent on the results of the standardised tests given to pupils in their last year at state or church run junior schools, the school population was then largely divided between grammar and secondary modern schools for their next five years' education. Bingley, though part of Bradford, has always had its own identity as a town, mainly thanks to its long history. Its name was entered in the Domesday Book, though then it was known as 'Binghelela'. Despite the efforts of many to drag it into the 21st century, an old atmosphere of yesteryear still pops its head up with hints of the town's proud past and ancient heritage. A well-worn bridge over the river at Beckfoot, the seclusion of its ancient parish church in Old Main Street and the elegant style of its town hall all help preserve the attractiveness of the place that the Victorians referred to as 'the throstle nest of old England'.

Left: One man does it all on the bus of today, but it used to take two to operate the trams and buses of yesteryear. The driver was isolated in his cab and separated from the passengers he conveyed. The conductor collected the fares and rang the bell to instruct his partner when to set off or when to pull up at the next stop. With a cry of 'Pass further down the bus, please', standing passengers were exhorted to squash closer together so that a few more could be squeezed on board. When no more could be fitted into this particular half pint pot, three rings told the driver that he could whiz past the next stop, much to the disgust on the faces of those waiting patiently in the queue. Driving was a solitary job and those of a quieter nature were well suited to the task, but the conductor had to be the more open sort of chap who could indulge in banter with the general public. He was also a friend to the old and infirm, helping them on and off with a cheery 'Mind how you go, love'.

Below: Whatever the nature of the injuries or, we hope, the lack of them, this was a very nasty accident. Shocked and stunned, a mixture of victims and witnesses stand around surveying the scene. Whether or not the West Yorkshire bus in the background was involved, we do not know, but this Model T Ford would be headed for the scrapyard. Road safety became a serious issue between the wars. At first, the novelty of the motor car meant that young men about town could whiz along the highways like some form of Mr Toad, tooting their hooters with scarves streaming along behind them as they peered through their goggles at the road ahead. There was a carefree abandon about driving that led to serious problems as more and more cars were rolled off the assembly lines. The ratio of fatalities to cars on the road was far worse in the 1930s than it is today and electrically controlled traffic lights, pedestrian crossings, cats' eyes and driving tests were introduced.

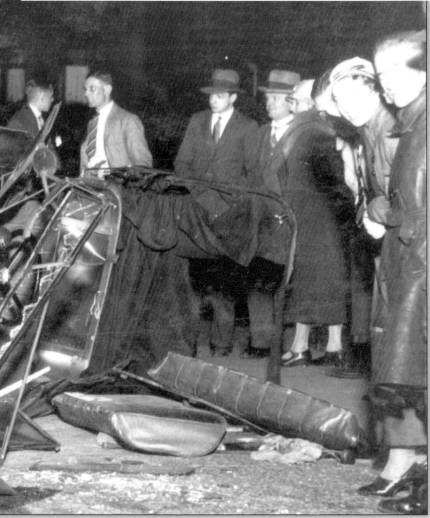

Above: The row of cars outside Bradford's Central Garage is a reminder of the days when we once had a thriving motor industry. Herbert Austin was one of the pioneers of this industry. Born in Buckinghamshire in 1866, his family settled in Wentworth, Yorkshire in the 1870s. Something of an adventurer, Austin worked for a while in Australia for the Wolseley Sheep Shearing Company, before returning to Britain as the manager of its outlet here. As an engineer, he turned his attention from fleeces to four wheels and helped design the first Wolseley cars. In 1905, he resigned and formed his own company and established the plant at Longbridge in the midlands that would grow into one of the largest manufacturing sites in the country. By 1910, nearly 1,000 workers were employed there and a night shift was found to be necessary. In the interwar years, the company went from strength to strength, being particularly popular with the middle and upper classes. The 16/18 models built just before the second world war were amongst the best sellers of that era. Herbert Austin died in 1941 as Lord Austin, Baron of Longbridge. The sign on the side of the garage further reminds us of the place held by British engineering in the history of commercial vehicles. Leyland Motors dated back to 1896, while Karrier was originally a Huddersfield firm founded by Herbert and Reginald Clayton.

SHOPPING SPREE

Although this photograph of Tom Green's Refreshment House is undated, the flags and decorations suggest that it might have connections with a national event, such as a coronation. The style of dress favoured by the women and children we can see might lead us in the direction of 1902, the year in which Edward VII was crowned, the year after his mother, Queen Victoria, passed away. The next coronation would take place in 1911 when Edward's son became George V. All we can be sure of is that this was Main Street in Bingley. Three centuries earlier, Bingley was just a quiet hamlet of one street with about 40 houses scattered on either side. The industrial revolution and developments circa 1800 changed all that as the woollen industry changed the face of the quiet, little market town into a hubbub of activity based upon the workings of the nearby mills. In the later years of the 19th century many people turned to the Bingley Building Society, formed in 1851, for assistance in looking after their greater wealth and providing funds for home buying and expansion. Even as our shopkeeper in the foreground looked out across the street a century ago, she must have enjoyed the quaint contradiction that was, and perhaps still is, our Bingley. The old has always rubbed shoulders with the new as farmlands run all the way up to factory walls and railway sidings and Tudor mullion windows look across at the sash windows of neo-Georgian semidetached suburbia.

Below: Only when walking from one end of the city to another do you fully appreciate that Bradford is a hilly district and shoppers need a good pair of lungs to get through the experience. This view down Darley Street, now a pedestrianised area, reinforces that description quite dramatically. Kirkgate Market, on the right, was an imposing edifice. It was built at a cost of £83,381 in 1878 to replace an earlier market. Here, shoppers were offered an impressive choice of produce right in the centre of the city, just opposite the tram and trolleybus stops outside the town hall. Its cast iron frame was most imposing, as were the huge figures of Pomona and Flora that graced the entrance arch. Pomona was the Roman goddess of fruit trees, orchards and gardens and is usually associated with abundance, while Flora represented flowers and the springtime. Closer to the camera is the former Central Library, while the old Savoy Cinema is just across the cobbled road. Situated next to Marks and Spencer, it rose five storeys above the pavement. Built in 1920, it was the largest of city centre cinemas with a seating capacity of 1,593.

Above: Burton's stood on this corner, close to the Darley Street entrance to Kirkgate Market. Younger readers might puzzle over the meaning of the 55/- sign. To those of us brought up on lsd, which is pounds, shillings and pence and not a hallucinatory dip into the swinging 60s, the price of 55 bob is straightforward enough. It translated in formal terms to £2 15s or £2.75 in today's money. However, this makes the advertisement most misleading if the price of a suit was in fact five guineas and not as the amount first suggested by the numbers we can see. A guinea was £1 1s, so, unless a price reduction was in force, the true cost of the clothing was £5 5s (£5.25). Burton's outfitters, 'the tailor of taste' as the slogan had it, was founded by Meshe Minsky, a Lithuanian Jew who came to Chesterfield in 1900. He adopted the surname of the town close to where he had established a small base. By 1910 he had opened four shops, but before long his business expanded to such a degree that he set up a huge factory in Leeds. In the 1920s and 1930s it seemed Burton was opening a new shop in a different town virtually every month.

Below: The British are a wonderfully patient people. As a tourist outside these shores, anyone who has waited for a bus, been stuck in a traffic jam or queued to get into a tourist attraction has had to experience the bad manners and impatience of the majority of our continental cousins. No orderly line for them, but a push and shove or an overtaking manoeuvre designed to alarm those of a cautious nature. Just look at the way that it should be done. The long crocodile snaking around the bus shelters in Forster Square is not just typical of the late 1940s, but of the English sangfroid that continues today. The trolley buses and trams were working side by side, but not for much longer as the latter were soon to be phased out. The covered bay was erected in 1939 and passengers were pleased with the protection it provided from the elements during the periods of inclement weather to which any northern traveller had to be hardened. Despite it being a chilly day, many women wore shortish skirts as clothing rationing restricted their fashion choice and it was not until the 1950s that they were able to indulge their taste for fuller, longer styles.

Right: The toy department at Brown Muff in 1933 was a magical place for a youngster to enter. All manner of teddy bears, dolls' houses, nurses' uniforms, embroidery kits and miniature cups and saucers were on display for girls to enjoy. The boys had the run of lead soldiers, Meccano, Hornby train sets, blow football and multi coloured glass marbles. It was like entering Aladdin's cave and there was so much to see and experience that a child could be lost in wonder in here for hours on end. The younger reader will get an idea of how nippers from those days marvelled at what they saw if he accompanies his grandpa to a toy museum today. Just watch the old man's eyes glaze over as he sees a replica of the first Dinky car that came on the market in the year that this scene was captured on film. Will adults in years to come go back in time and reminisce in the same way about their first Pacman, Super Mario or Donkey Kong computer game? Call us cynics, but we doubt it because the world of toys, before the PlayStation or X Box hit the shops, was wrapped up in a dreamy package where our imagination took us on a magical trip that was not restricted by the confines built into the parameters determined by the writers of computer software.

Top right: Members of the armed forces in 1940 knew that 14 February 1940 was not too far away and it was important that they got a card for their loved ones as Valentine's Day offered an opportunity to reinforce an old love and, perhaps, to forge a

new one. Some cheeky lads did both! The assistant was a patient lass, enjoying the banter of the young men as they flirted with her, while at the same time professing undying love for some sweetheart far away. Valentines were usually straight forward messages of love and devotion, often written in rather twee rhyming couplets. Covered in hearts, flowers and pictorial bows, they offered an air of mystery blended with simplicity. Few of them were humorous and none whatsoever were smutty. Men valued ladies far too highly to resort to such tactics. They addressed their envelopes to Doris or Dorothy, Edith or Evelyn and never signed them. It was usual practice to disguise the sender's handwriting.

Occupying a prominent position on Town Hall Square, the Burton building informed everybody that it would 'dress you'. Market Street bends away past Burton's, with Thornton Road leading off to the left. The camera was pointing along Tyrell Street towards the Wool Exchange, a grand example of both the architecture and history that helped make Bradford great. The building reflects the great wealth and importance which Bradford had gained

from the wool trade by the middle of the 19th century. Architects Lockwood and Mawson won the open competition for its design in 1857, though it was not until 1864 that the foundation stone was laid by Prime Minister, Lord Palmerston.

Between the ground floor arches are carved portraits of notable people and, by the entrance, statues of Bishop Blaise, the patron saint of woolcombers, and King Edward III who greatly promoted the wool trade.

Above: Leeds Road was heavy with traffic on 15 April 1954. It was late in the afternoon and both shoppers and office workers had packed up for the day and were making their way home. Some would return later on to have a night out at the Ritz, the cinema on the left. 'Going to the flicks' was still an important part of our social life in those days. Television was still in its infancy and the stars of the silver screen attracted us to a diversion that was one of high spots of the week. You got value for money, too, as there was usually a double bill of movies, some sort of comedy short or a cartoon, perhaps a travel feature and a Pathé or Movietone newsreel. All this for less than a couple of bob made it a good night out. The whole programme often began at teatime and continued through until about 10 o'clock and offered the opportunity for a quaint method of watching a film that seems almost unique to the British. Quite often, a customer would arrive and take a seat part way through the action, watch the whole screening of programmes and then depart when the first story reached the bit where he had come in. This meant that the film had been viewed with the ending being revealed before the cinemagoer knew how it had begun. Bizarre, but we did it. Of course, it did not matter if you came as a courting couple because you would not be watching the screen, would you?

Above: The pedestrian underpass at Petergate, with its John Menzies shop, was brightly lit and looked almost brand, spanking new, as indeed it should in 1967. The regeneration of the city centre brought about the need to provide people with a safe way to cross the remodelled roads. Dodging over roundabouts or trying to beat the traffic lights was asking for trouble. However, as the years went by, many of us became wary of some of the subways in the city as they started to look dowdy and could be unnerving for those out on their own. Opinion was divided and the tone of letters to the local press reflected this.

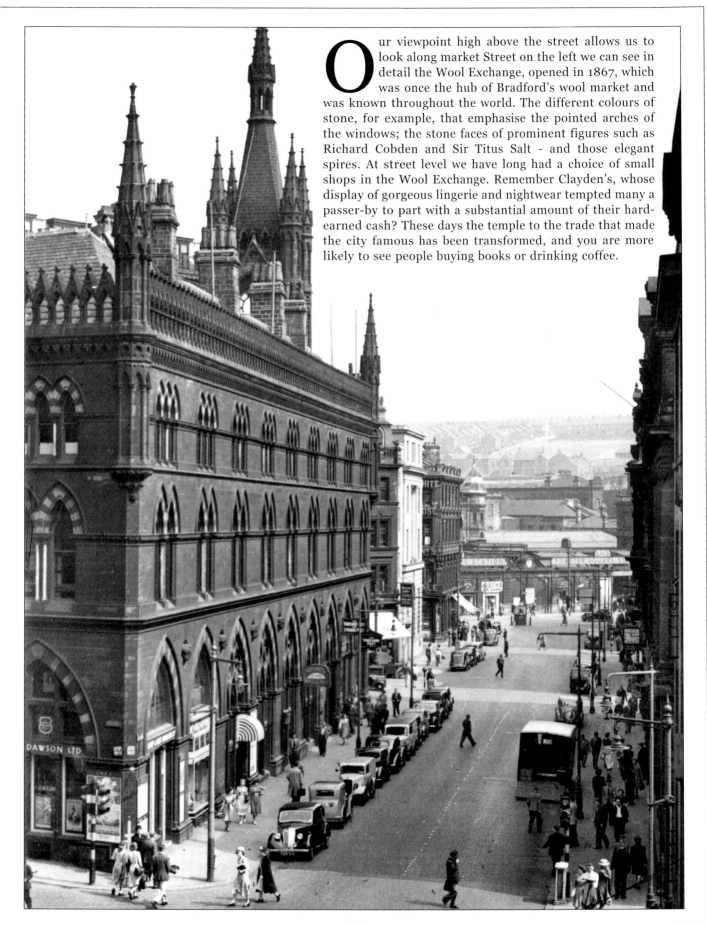

Our viewpoint high above the street allows us to look along market Street on the left we can see in detail the Wool Exchange, opened in 1867, which was once the hub of Bradford's wool market and was known throughout the world. The different colours of stone, for example, that emphasise the pointed arches of the windows; the stone faces of prominent figures such as Richard Cobden and Sir Titus Salt - and those elegant spires. At street level we have long had a choice of small shops in the Wool Exchange. Remember Clayden's, whose display of gorgeous lingerie and nightwear tempted many a passer-by to part with a substantial amount of their hard-earned cash? These days the temple to the trade that made the city famous has been transformed, and you are more likely to see people buying books or drinking coffee.

Above and top right: Busby's department store offered more than just clothing, furniture and everyday items. It also catered for the finer grooming needs that discerning ladies could enjoy. Its hairdressing salon offered both comfort and deferential attention. The lounge and waiting area was tastefully appointed so that they could relax while waiting to go through for their perm. Ancient Egyptians used to curl their hair by wrapping strands tightly around sticks and then applying warm mud that was scraped off later. Things did not seem to have moved on much when, in 1906, the German Karl Nessler introduced his technique for a permanent wave that relied on a mixture of water and cow's urine. However, with the widespread introduction of electricity, curls were produced by wrapping hair in a spiral around rods connected to a machine with an electric heating device. Initially, these were bulky contraptions and none too safe, as testified by a number of scalded scalps. In 1938, Arnold F. Willatt invented the cold wave, the precursor to the modern perm. It used no machines and no heat. The hair was wrapped on rods and a reduction lotion was applied. After the second world war, advertisers went to town pushing their products. One of the best remembered is the one for Toni. It showed two lookalikes and asked if we could tell which twin had the Toni. Pins and curlers were all the rage, but it was only the lower classes who wore them when out and about. Posher folk went to Busby's to dine in some elegance as can be seen in the picture top right. The current trend of fast food and greasy spoons was not for the clientele who patronised the handsome establishment where it promised 'everyone a friendly welcome'. No-one walked into the restaurant in anything other than smart attire. When Busby's was in its prime the thought of a man without a tie or jacket was mind boggling and if a lady entered in a pair of slacks or without her hat on, then the conclusion was obvious, she was no lady. This did not mean that the store was the prerogative of the middle classes, just that everybody had a sense of what was right in the way they dressed in the middle years of the last century. A working class man might have a slightly shiny suit, but it was still a suit after all and he had his own brand of formal headgear in the cloth cap. Lunching at Busby's was an important occasion and one to be treated with some sense of decorum.

become known for its red light district and street riots, but it once had a much more reputable quality with its mix of large merchants' villas and textile workers' terraced properties. Thomas Campbell Hope (1834-1916) was the architect who had a major influence on the design and layout of the buildings in this area as a residential suburb. Many retail businesses flourished on its streets, serving a public who had some degree of financial security. One of the most memorable was the large department store on Manningham Lane. Advertising itself as 'The store with the friendly welcome', Busby's was a place to where shoppers flocked from far and wide. It was on the important thoroughfare from Keighley to Skipton and attracted Kirkgate retailer Ernest W Busby to move his business here in 1908. His premises were in the Royal Arcade, built in 1897, originally conceived as a set of individual shops with living accommodation above. In later years the store was owned by Debenhams before closing in 1978 and being burned down a year later.

Below: The district of Manningham is home to Lister Park, donated to the city by the Victorian industrialist, Samuel Lister in 1870. Voted Britain's best park in 2006, it is also the home of Cartwright Hall, a prestigious art gallery. Lister's Mill is now a large block of apartments that have become popular with couples and single professionals. In more recent times, Manningham has

ON THE ROAD

If you think that bouncy castles were in use during the last war, then this one had a potentially nasty surprise in store. The bag on top of the Morris Commercial was filled with gas. The vehicle had been converted to use this as a fuel. Petrol rationing was introduced just a couple of weeks after the outbreak of war and stayed with us for over a decade. The Garden Dairy decided to keep its fleet of lorries on the road by using this mind boggling method of fuel storage. The drivers must have had nerves of steel to bowl along the roads with such a potential fireball sitting above their heads. Can you imagine the reaction of the health and safety executive in modern Britain? But, during the war it was a case of make do and mend. The dairy's slogan 'Rich milk made safe' referred to the treatment it had received during processing when transferring milk from churns into bottles for home consumption. It was only in 1922 that the Milk and Dairies Act tightened up on production and distribution methods.

SAFETY FIRST. BOTTLED AT THE GARDEN DAIRY.

STERILIZED MILK

RICH MILK MADE SAFE

II

Below: Skipton regards itself as the gateway to the Dales and some of the picturesque scenery around the North Yorkshire town can be glimpsed in the background. To the right of the van, the driver seems to be speaking into the microphone to an audience that might just have consisted of seven sheep and a couple of cows. The company, a plumbing, glazing, electrical and decorating contractor that began in 1870, was based at 54 High Street, later to become Boot's. The founder's name suggests that the man in the picture might just have been practising for a role as a crooner. Christened George Harrison Mason, he might just have inspired the naming of a future Beatle who would be born not too long after this photograph was taken. The man at the microphone, although obviously not intending to launch into 'Smoke gets in your eyes', really does look like one of the crooners who entertained our parents and grandparents with such numbers. Whispering Jack Smith, Rudy Vallee and Bing Crosby were just a few of those who adopted a static pose behind the microphone and wowed live and record audiences with their voices. The van in the photograph was just the sort that was often used by local firms to drive the streets, advertising their wares to the public via the loudspeakers mounted on top.

Above: Offering the very latest technology in chromium plating, the Sanda Metal Company could drive its van around as a first hand advertisement for some of its own products. It even produced the very number plate attached to its vehicle. Based at 104-106 Rook Lane, Dudley Hill, where the road now forms a link for traffic from the northbound A650 for traffic heading clockwise onto the ring road, Sanda's chromium plating operation was a growing business during the interwar years.

Right: The delightful aroma of bread being baked and custard slices fresh from the ovens comes back, not to mind, but to nose with this photograph. Asa Nicholson, then a quarryman, turned his hand to bakery during a period of unemployment in the harsh winter of 1898. With the prompting of his sister, Nicholson contacted a Halifax man who provided him with the training that assisted in the establishment of a business that initially sold the produce from door to door. His oat bread was a particular delicacy that sold like the hot cakes he later made in the bakery he set up at Bottomley Holes. As the business grew, Asa took his sons in with him during the 1920s. By 1947, new premises were needed and the firm moved to Oats Royd, Keelham. For many years, confectionery sales were supplemented by those made

out of a retail van, such as this 1929 model. The last driver of one of these retired in 1988. The company now includes Asa's great grandson as part of the management team.

Left: Parked up on Midland Road, near Thorncliffe Road, the trio of 1930s' vans belonged to Gott's Pops. Somewhat dubiously advertised as 'the new health sweet', the company would be unlikely to get away with such a claim in the modern climate of advertising standards. Clientele from that era, though, would have literally swallowed the message along with the sweets.

Below right: Burton still advertises itself as being 'the tailor of taste'. Still, if you have a good slogan, why ditch it? Many clothing companies have come up with catchy jingles and sayings that have been retained in our memories as part of our heritage. John Collier was 'the window to watch', Rael Brook poplin was 'the shirt you don't iron' and Henry Price even gave up his own name to become quite simply 'the fifty shilling tailor'. The chromium plating and lettering on this delivery vehicle was provided by Bradford's Sanda Metal Company. Montague Burton's company had become well established during the years in between the two world wars. Burton moved production from Chesterfield to Leeds and by 1925 had enough business to expand to the huge factory on Hobson Road in that city where he employed up to 10,000 workers. The huge canteen could feed as many as 7,000 in one sitting. Even a major order was turned round within a week and by the start of World War II he was clothing a quarter of British males. The expression, 'the full Monty', referred to a three piece suit and had nothing to do with male strippers from Sheffield, on our screens in 1997.

WORKING LIFE

The modern fire station at Bingley was constructed in 1972 on Keighley Road. However, from the turn of the 20th century until then, the local fire brigade worked out of premises on Market Street that have been a health centre and a warehouse since its closure. For the last few years it has served as a wine bar. These men were among the first firefighters to be based at that site and posed for their photograph displaying some

of the advanced equipment available to them at the time. Their horsedrawn appliance might not have offered the speediest of responses, but the men could be guaranteed to attack any incident with professionalism and bravery once they arrived on the scene. The brass helmets they wore were phased out after several dangerous incidents. When first introduced, they provided good head protection, but as more and more properties were equipped with electricity, it was painfully discovered that the helmets provided an unfortunately good conduction of electricity if they came into contact with exposed wiring. This, linked with the amount of water that might be around, soon meant that the helmets were consigned to the museum and only ever produced on ceremonial occasions in the future. The photograph was taken outside Bingley Town Hall, the former Springhead mansion house in Myrtle Park that has been there since 1770.

Below: What we see here is the 1950s' version of Jamie Oliver's healthy eating regime for the school meal service as rice pudding and soup are loaded into large containers. As part of the postwar Labour government's social welfare scheme, all schools were expected to provide a nourishing dinner for their pupils. Those families on low incomes were given free meals, but even those who could afford to pay found that their food was subsidised. Some establishments had their own kitchens, while others relied on centrally prepared meals that were sent out in vans across the borough. Oh the joys of school dinners in those days that we can now look back on. The spuds usually contained blackened areas that forced a pupil to close his eyes as he forced them down, the vegetables were as well stewed as the prunes that followed. Anyone brought up in that era has never again tasted semolina or tapioca pudding since. The true horror of some of those meals was reinforced by teachers on dinner duty who took it in turns to force us all to clear our plates as it was considered a crime in those austere times to waste a single mouthful. The only saving grace of the welfare thrust came in the morning when we got a small bottle of milk.

Right: Work began at first dawn for mill workers. To ensure that they were roused from their slumbers, knocker-ups were employed to get them out of bed. This old woman used an implement to give the front door a sharp rap, while others carried long poles so that they good tap on the glass of the bedroom window. The knocker-ups were paid a miniscule amount for their work. The people entrusted with getting the workforce to their looms on time were sometimes paid by those who they roused, while others were in the employ of the mill owners. Failure to attend work on time meant a loss of wages for one side and a dip in production for the other, so both benefited from the sound of a rat-a-tat every

morning. The conundrum of who knocked up the knocker-up, though, has never been answered. It is probably to be found alongside the answer to the question of how a road gritter gets to work. Once the family had been roused, the arduous day began. Long lines of workers trudged across the cobbles and setts, their clogs sparking as they went, in a scene that might have inspired an LS Lowry painting or song about 'Matchstalk men and matchstalk cats and dogs'.

Below: The habit of calling a female teacher 'Miss' came about from the marital status of such a woman. Formal education was in the hands of the spinster who was expected to vacate her position when she married. A woman's place as a wife was in the home, cooking and cleaning and looking after her husband and children. We can only wonder what this schoolmistress made of it all in 1914. As her class of children at Usher Street Infant School, East Bowling gazed into the camera, how many of them had an inkling that they would lose a father, elder brother or uncle over the next few years? It is unlikely that any of these little ones is still with us, but perhaps some reader might recognise a forefather among the assembled group.

Below: During the last war we had an official Women's Land Army that, at its peak, had 80,000 members. Founded in the first world war, it came into its own in 1940 as 45,000 men had left the land to join the armed forces and other war related occupations. These men, however, were not part of that particular army, though they applied themselves to haymaking at Westwood Farm. This was part of their rehabilitation as they spent time at the nearby hospital recovering from wounds they had received at the front. Getting back into good physical shape was part of the plan and there was nothing better than hard graft to help them achieve this. The work also contributed to the war effort and helped the men's own sense of well being in being able to 'do their bit' as a number were also recuperating from battle fatigue. It was a sign of the times that, even when involved in physical tasks, men still dressed in jackets, until it became too warm and they were eventually discarded.

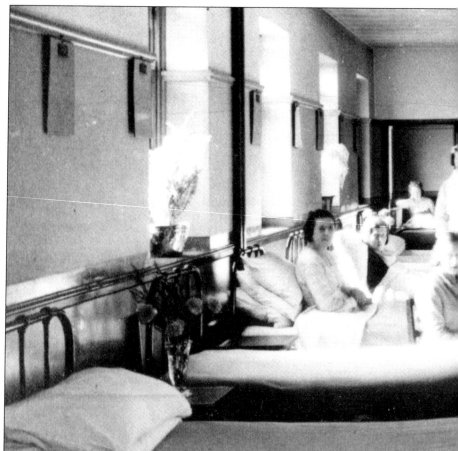

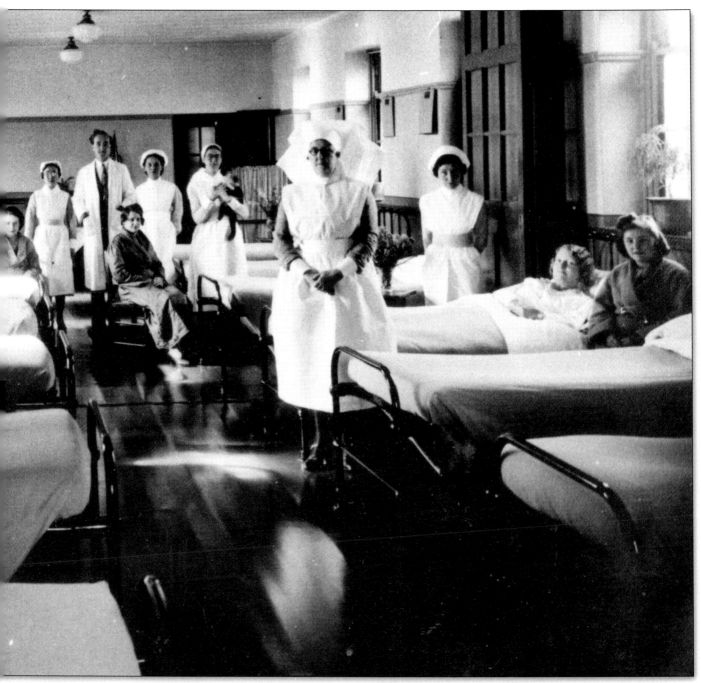

Above: This wartime picture of a women's ward at Westwood Hospital shows some of the casualties who were cared for here during the early 1940s. Although some might have been in uniform when they were injured, most of the female patients were civilian casualties of the Nazi bombing raids. The hospital was originally designated as an institution for women suffering from mental illness, catering for 34 inmates when it opened in 1918 in the former Westwood House at Clayton Heights. This was a year after Ashfield House at Thornton opened on 6 June 1917. Somewhat unsympathetically to the modern way of thinking, it was called the Ashfield House Mental Deficiency Hospital and helped the plight of mentally handicapped boys. It was the first of its kind to be provided by a municipality. Westwood grew in size during the 1920s as more land was acquired and buildings added. The new Westwood Institution opened on 28 July 1933, with facilities for both sexes. During the war, some 300 inmates were transferred elsewhere and the buildings were converted to serve as a military hospital that could deal with 600 patients at a time. Over 7,000 service casualties and 1,200 civilians were treated here before the hospital was returned to the Corporation Mental Health Authority in September 1945. The doctors and nurses had more than done their bit for the war effort.

Above: It was once not only acceptable to be a housewife, but decidedly desirable. Long before the term became non-pc, young women aspired to getting a husband and spending their time as homemakers. Perish the man who might suggest that a woman's place is at the kitchen sink or behind a vacuum cleaner in the 21st century. In the 1930s, housework was a time consuming chore. Clothes were washed by hand and required hard work with the dolly tub, posser, washboard and mangle. Pegging out or drying on the maiden hoisted high by a pulley all took time. Food was cooked on open ranges and had to be bought several times a week as perishable items could only be stored in cold larders as fridges were expensive and the technology involving them was comparatively primitive. Floors were scrubbed and carpets beaten, so that when the man in the house returned from his day at the office or at the workbench his home was spotless and his missus exhausted. Little wonder that these ladies had flocked to view a demonstration of modern kitchen appliances that might ease their load.

Above: In a similar vein Bradford Corporation Gas Department was trying to drum up custom for itself with this simple display that used one of its own trucks as a float. The department had a long history, dating from 1820 and continuing through to 1969. It looks hilarious now to those of us in our space age kitchens, but these were once the most modern of appliances.

Below: Henry Ford invented the assembly line as a way of speeding up production, but it should have been a smoother process than the version adopted at this assembly plant at Five Lane Ends. Benjamin and William Jowett founded their car company at Idle, between Norman Lane and Bradford Road, in 1906. Although they had built a prototype engine in 1899, the brothers began business as cycle manufacturers, but soon went into car manufacture. During the Great War, the Jowetts produced munitions, before returning to their first love. Successfully expanding the business during the 1930s, the company turned again to war work at the start of the 1940s. By then, the founders had retired and after the war production resumed with the focus on the Jowett Javelin, an upmarket saloon capable of 80 mph. The workers in this photograph are assembling examples of these. In 1950, the sporty Jupiter was added to the range. Unfortunately for all concerned, the management of the company overestimated sales demand. Cheaper family saloons, although not necessarily superior in design, from Ford, Austin and Morris provided fierce competition. Jowett's stockpiled large numbers of cars and cash flow became an insurmountable problem. The company closed in 1954 and the factory was sold to a company manufacturing aircraft parts.

Above: Unemployment hit the working classes hard during the 1930s as the number out of work spiralled above 3 million at one stage. The textile trade suffered as demand fell and costs increased. The outbreak of World War II brought some respite for the industry, though it was hardly a time for celebration. The largely female staff tended the machines that produced huge volumes of fabric for parachutes, battledresses, camouflage cloths and blankets. In the immediate postwar years, the industry rallied for a while as new manmade fabrics were introduced, but it was merely a temporary recovery largely down to households refurbishing homes that had seen little improvement in recent times. By the 1950s, when these overlookers at Lister's Manningham Mills checked their figures, the industry was once more on the way down. Cheap imports from abroad hit the traditional mill towns of the north quite badly. A history of poor investment in updating equipment and the birth of new technology in the 1960s and 70s helped toll the death knell for the majority of firms. Lister's once provided velvets and silks for houses and palaces across the world, but in 1992 it all ended.

Below left: This busy Bradford spinning mill was turning out yarn and cloth in this scene taken from the early 1950s. The noise of the machines was one of the main problems for the workforce who, at times, could hardly hear themselves speak above the racket. In some parts of the mill it was pointless tuning in to 'Workers' Playtime' as you couldn't make out a word that Ken Platt was saying about not taking his coat off because he wasn't stopping or that Jimmy Young was warbling about as he sang that he was 'Too Young'. At least it was better than before the war when the noise was so bad that the workforce was overwhelmed at the roar and all it could hear was a ringing in the ears for the whole evening after the end of the shift. Of course, people adjusted and learned to converse despite the row. Although they didn't realise it, many adopted a lot of lip reading techniques. Some girls shut out the noise by simply daydreaming and thinking about the coming weekend. Perhaps this lass in the foreground was mooning over the lad she had met at the dancehall last week. Would he walk her home again this Saturday?

Below: You can almost hear Miriam Karlin shout 'Everybody out' to Peter Jones' annoyance in the early 1960s' television sitcom 'The Rag Trade', but this sewing shop is seen in the 1940s and women and trade unions did not mix well at that time. Although machinists were skilled practitioners in their trade, many had learned the skill long before they were old enough to work. Most homes had a sewing machine, more often than not a Singer, on which they treadled away as the needle pushed up and down through the material that was fed through. Sewing, whether for pleasure and decoration as embroidery or out of necessity in running up curtains, making clothing or mending dad's overalls, was part and parcel of a girl's domestic education. During the war, such women provided a vital back up to the men at the front. They produced thousand upon thousand of uniforms, shirts, sweaters, blankets and all manner of other necessary items from parachutes to bed linen as part of their contribution to the war. There was no thought of downing tools because of some minor problem as it was a case of pulling together for the common good.

Bradford College
'Pioneers in Education 1832 - 2007'

The roots of Bradford College can be found in the Bradford Mechanics Institute. The first institute was founded by radicals in 1825 but soon closed due to the unpopularity of their views amongst the middle-classes.

Led by the 26 year old Baptist Joseph Farrar, along with James Acworth and Dr Steadman, Quakers, John Hustler and Henry Harris and Congregationalists, Sir Titus Salt and Robert Milligan, it opened its first premises in March 1832 in Piccadilly and by 1839 moved to larger premises in Wells Street.

Teachers were voluntary and funds depended upon fees raised from lectures, exhibitions, excursions and concerts. The focus was on essential skills – Writing and Arithmetic with evening classes in Literature, History and the Popular Sciences. By 1863, however, it had its own 'School of Industrial Design and Art' – the nucleus of technical education - and was employing its first paid, fully qualified teachers.

The textile industry did not support the institute in its early days, preferring to keep trade secrets in-house. Bradford's industrialists began to come on board in the years following the Paris exhibition in 1867, which popularised French fashions and demanded greater artistry. Local industrialists joined forces with the Council of the Mechanics Institute and the Chamber of Commerce where Sir Henry Mitchell, knighted for his services to education, was instrumental in promoting the idea of technical education to feed the local industry.

Funds poured in, starting with £2,000 as a guaranteed sum, boosted by Sir Henry Mitchell, Henry Ripley, Sir Titus Salt and other local industrialists. A new 'Italianate' building was erected at the corner of Tyrell Street, Bridge Street and Market Street. The Technical School was born: its cost was £23,500. On 2nd October 1871, Bradford MP WE Forster declared it open. It had classrooms for over 700 students, an art room, a lecture room with 1,500 seats, a saloon seating 350 for sales, meetings, exhibitions and speakers, and a

City of London, laid the foundation stone. The design of the building was 'state of the art' – with public grand rooms at the front of the building and large, airy teaching and learning areas featuring the latest ventilation and heating systems and flushing toilets. It cost £37,000.

The Bradford Technical School was unique in its direct relevance to the textile and mechanical industries associated not only with Bradford – but to the country as a whole.

On 23rd June 1882, the then Prince and Princess of Wales (later King Edward VII and Queen Alexandra) travelled to Bradford to open the new Technical School.

Ceremonial arches were erected along the processional route from Saltaire where the Royal couple were to stay with Mr Titus Salt, son of Sir Titus Salt. Caterers were dispatched as far as London to source the best strawberries for the grand lunch hosted by Sir Henry Mitchell. An exhibition of the finest art, textiles and machine innovations was mounted. Bradford craftsmen produced their best examples of wood and soft furnishings for the reading rooms and public rooms on the ground floor.

Top left: Where it all began at the Bradford Mechanical Institute. **Left, above and below:** Celebrations for the opening of the Technical College, (below) by the then Prince and Princess of Wales, above.

library with precisely 9,935 books. Sir Henry Mitchell was the first Council President of the Mechanics Institute in its new premises.

Scholarships were available to able students, with free elementary evening classes. The day portfolio included Applied Mechanics, Bookkeeping, Chemistry, Music, Drawing, Modern European Languages, Metallurgy, Literature, Politics, Drawing, History and Geography.

By 1874 a small building trades school had moved in from Godwin Street – to be recognised as the Weaving School in 1877.

Some 250 students were enrolled at the outset and the Council realised that a new building was now required. The Mayor of Bradford, Mr Briggs Priestley, rallied key industrialists who raised £17,000 towards the building fund – soon boosted by a further £3,000 from the Clothworkers' Company of London and by local contributions.

A year later Bradford Council bought an acre of land at the junction of Great Horton Road and Carlton Street. Designs were invited from architects for a new Technical School and, from 16 entries, Mr Thomas C Hope of Messrs Hope & Jardine was appointed.

In June 1880, Lt. Col John Britten, the Master of the Worshipful Company of Clothworkers of the

Bradford people packed the processional route and Great Horton Road outside the School. Street parties went on long into the night.

Sir Henry Mitchell was the first President of the Representative Council governing the new institution. He and his fellow founders in the early days largely financed the institution and its expansion themselves. In 1883, Day Schools, with independent Heads were established to offer daytime classes in Textile Industries, Engineering, Dyeing and Art. Evening classes in technical subjects were launched at the start of the September term that year. By 1884, demand was so high that a second chemical laboratory was provided. As growth continued an additional floor had to be added to the side wing of the building.

Local residents were not all pleased. Balls held at the School led residents to protest about the noise of cab traffic opposite their houses on Carlton Street, and to request that when dances were held, the main public door should be used instead.

Following the 1889 Technical Instruction Act and the 1890 Local Taxation Act the local Council provided some grants to assist the School. The Trust Deed was amended to include representation of the Bradford Council on the Corporation of the School.

In the 1890s the Technical School was renamed Bradford Technical College. By 1899, when control of the College passed to Bradford Corporation, the priority was to extend accommodation and provide much needed financial assistance. The Day Science School closed and the Department of Art became a separate College of Art in 1904, and settled in the Mannville New Connection Chapel (currently the Grove Library) on the other side of the main road. Planned new buildings for the Textiles Department and boiler, engine, power and plant house progressed slowly, and it wasn't until October 1911 that Lord Rotherham opened these premises on Carlton Street. They included teaching areas for washing, carding, combing, spinning, weaving, dyeing and finishing.

During the First World War hundreds of students and staff lost their lives but, after the war, expansion continued. Land was purchased for a new Engineering block in 1920 and by 1922 another state-of-the-art building was opened. Mechanical Engineering and Civil Engineering made up two separate departments. The Departments of Electrical and

Botany swelled the prospectus offering, followed by the Department of Commerce and Banking in 1925 and the Department of Pharmacy in 1927.

In 1930 work began to extend the main building by erecting a three-storey adjoining wing and adding a two-storey building at the back of the College. In 1933 the Earl of Athlone opened what became known as the Athlone Wing.

The 1930s ended with the provision of further extensions to house classrooms and workshops for the Mechanical, Electrical, Chemistry, Dyeing and Physics department. Study continued to be as popular as ever during the Second World War. The 1944 Education Act, which called upon local authorities to provide Adult Education facilities, added to demand. Senior Technical Institutes existed at Belle Vue, Carlton and Hanson, along with other domestic and evening institutes: these were boosted in 1946 by day release classes for young employees to include vocational courses in Industry and Commerce.

The Government proposed the introduction of CATS (Colleges of Advanced Technology) in a 1956 White Paper. CATS were to deliver expanded technical education aligned with plans to expand technology provision within certain University Departments. One of the first eight CATs in the country was created at Bradford Technical College in 1957, to train technologists bound for responsible industrial

positions in Design, Production, Research and Administration. This College – the nucleus of the University that was to come - was still administered by the local authority. By 1962, it was to receive its funds through the University Grants Committee and pass from the local authority to the Ministry of Education – and in 1966 it was to receive its Charter as a University, with the Rt. Hon Harold Wilson, the Prime Minister, becoming its first Chancellor.

The Technical College remained separate, continuing its own expansion. By 1959 the College had absorbed the three Senior Technical Institutes, Belle Vue, Hanson and Carlton and had applied to build new premises in Great Horton Road. Approval was granted and Alderman Revis Barber opened the Westbrook extensions in 1965. By 1967, the next phase of the Westbrook extension had begun and opened to students in 1969. It was named the Kent Wing when the Duchess of Kent formally opened the new premises in 1972.

In September 1973, the Bradford Technical College and the Regional College of Art united to form a new College, The Bradford College of Art and Technology, with a single Principal for both institutions and larger premises for the

Top left, left and below: Views inside the new Technical College of 1892: The Hall, top left, Engineering, below left and the Mechanical Laboratory, below.

Art College. Alderman Doris Birdsall unveiled a plaque in the Westbrook building to mark the occasion and the new name – soon to be followed by another new name, another plaque and another first for Bradford. In April 1975, The Bradford College of Art and Technology and the Margaret McMillan College of Education merged, the latter being named 'Trinity Building'. The merger was the first in the country to combine Colleges of Art, Technology and Teacher Training. The student numbers of over 20,000 and staff numbers of over 400 underlined its significance. When Lord Crowther-Hunt, Minister of State for Further and Higher Education, unveiled the further plaque, it announced the opening of the newly named 'Bradford College'.

In 1974 the Bradford Metropolitan Council had been formed, taking in neighbouring Ilkley, Shipley, Keighley and Bingley. Bradford College delivered courses to the Wharfedale area, creating 'Bradford & Ilkley College' with bases in Burley in Wharfedale and Ilkley.

Historic Bradford bases formed the main Adult Education Centres at Joseph Nutter House (the former orphanage for boys set up by Christopher Pratt's apprentice, Joseph Nutter) Bolton Royd (a house built by the Horsfall brothers of the Chartist riots and extended to an elaborate family home), Burley Grange (originally home of the Hodgsons) and Wells House, Ilkley (an original 1859 hydrotherapy spa).

By the 1990s, Bradford College was one of the largest Further and Higher Education institutions in the country, boasting enrolments of up to 36,000 students and offering a portfolio across a wide range of provision from the Sixth Form Centre, to Vocational and Adult courses with a part and full-time Further and Higher Education provision across several schools. International links were growing with College partnerships

Top: The Technology Laboratory, 1892. **Left and above:** *Bolton Royd (left) and Joseph Nutter House, two historic building which based main adult education centres.*

extending to the Pacific Rim and students from all over the world attending summer schools and Further and Higher Education courses. On the 1st April 1993, the College became incorporated under the Further and Higher Education Act of 1992 and once again was governed by its own body of Governors, drawn from local businesses and the local community with representation from students and staff. As distance-learning began to grow, central funding changes began to re-shape Adult Education and the new agenda for skills became a priority, the College retained smaller bases in Wharfedale and began to launch new city-centre facing education centres in Bradford and district, still delivering its large portfolio from its city centre base and still working with its partners internationally – and once again using its best known name 'Bradford College'.

Bradford College entered the 21st century with a bold new 'big B' brand. The College has also unveiled a five year programme to develop a campus of iconic world class buildings that will inspire its students for many years to come. The first female Principal, Michele Sutton joined representatives of Bradford Metropolitan Council to complete an Asian tour of India, Pakistan and Thailand, extending the College's international appeal to bring even more students to Bradford from all over the world.

The College continues the pioneering work that has earned so many 'firsts' for Bradford and is once again seeking its own degree awarding powers. The College houses the UK Women's Resource Centre to encourage women into Science, Engineering & Technology; the successful northern Teacher Training Agency; the Early Years Test Centre; the WOW Academy (for new media and technology); the Bradford School of Arts and Media and the Yorkshire Craft Centre; the Bradford School of Business and Law; the McMillan School of Teaching, Health and Care; and 'Level 6' – popular with locals who sample the skills of our Catering, Leisure and Hair and Beauty students.

The Mechanics Institute attracted students from around the world to learn the techniques that were required of the woollen trade. Today Bradford College offers a portfolio that also attracts students from all over the globe, with courses delivered in key city venues.

On the 23rd June 2007 the College Principal, Governors, Lord Mayor, chief guests including Sir Digby Jones, Government Skills Envoy and former director-general of the CBI and Sir Clive Woodward, Elite Performance Director of the British Olympic Association and Sponsors will lay the foundation stone for the new Construction, Engineering and Sports Building. Simultaneously guests will gather in the former Technical School for it's 125th Anniversary celebrations.

The two events will unite for the reception, entertainment and lunch including the official renaming of the hall in the Old Building. The hall will be named after Sir Henry Mitchell.

This very special event will launch a year of celebration marking 175 years of providing Further and Higher Education to the City of Bradford. It will be an occasion on which the College will be justly proud.

*Top: At work in Multimedia Studies. **Left:** Arkwright Halls of Residence. The College leases 200 bedrooms from Arkwright Halls which are situated in Blocks F, G and H, built in 2004. **Below:** Doris Birdsall Halls of Residence. Built in 1998 it comprises 60 en-suite bedrooms designed as 5-bedroom, self-contained flats with shared kitchen facilities.*

CarnaudMetalBox Engineering
The Firm that Put the Can in Can Do

Dockfield Road, Shipley is home to the firm of CarnaudMetalBox Engineering. Since the 1970s it has been a major manufacturer of a range of equipment for two-piece can manufacture for the can-making industry throughout the world.

The CarnaudMetalbox name however, has only been in use since 1986: the roots of the business go back much further. Its direct predecessor, the Metal Box Company, was created in 1930, whilst the origins of that company's Shipley branch can be traced back to the mid 19th century and the firm of Lee & Crabtree Ltd.

Above: Founders, James Denby Lee and James Crabtree.
Below: Outlined is an aerial view of the original factory.

Amongst the earliest surviving records of the firm of Lee & Crabtree is a cashbook dating from 1853 in which is recorded the fact that the wage bill at the time was just £14 a month. Over the following century the number of employees would grow to over 400 and its wages bill multiply more than a thousand fold.

The small firm founded by James Denby Lee and James Crabtree in the reign of Queen Victoria was solely concerned with the manufacture of weaving looms and textile machinery at a time when England supplied textiles to the whole world. It was not until after the death of both founders that the production of presses and sheet metal working machinery began.

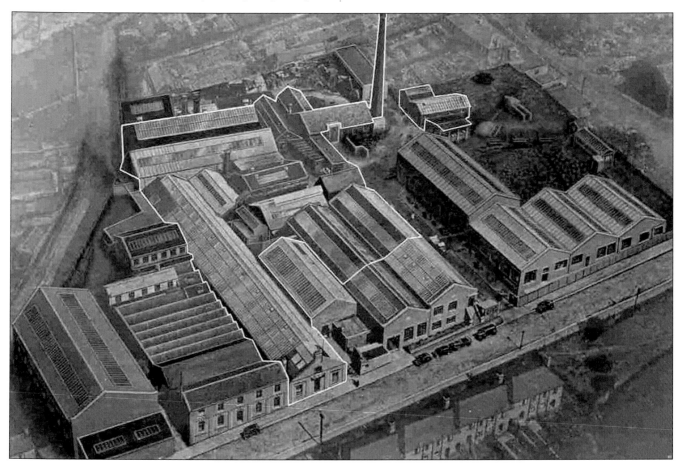

In 1870 the company produced what is thought to be the very first household washing machine which was demonstrated for three weeks in Shipley Market Place. It would be nice to record that this notable piece of enterprise met with success, but unfortunately the project was ahead of its time; although the inhabitants of Shipley and Windhill took full advantage of the opportunity to have their washing done free of charge, no buyers were found and the project was abandoned.

In the early days the company occupied premises at Valley Road, Windhill and later in Rhodes Place Shipley. On 28th December 1875 land and buildings covering an area of over 9,000 square yards were bought at Wrose Brow Road which would form the nucleus of a new factory.

James Denby Lee died in 1875, and when James Crabtree died eight years later his son William Arthur Crabtree was only sixteen years old. The business was therefore managed for the next five years by an uncle, Thomas Crabtree, on behalf of his nephew and his own son David Crabtree.

It was during this period that the manufacture of press tools and sheet metal working machinery began, when in 1887 Albert Shaw joined the firm. Albert Shaw and William Clark were for many years respectively manager and chief foreman of the press tool section of the firm, and the successful development of this side of the business owed much to their skill and expertise. From then until 1921 there were two distinct sections to Lee & Crabtree: one concerned with looms and other textile machinery, and the other devoted to the production of presses, press tools and sheet metal working machinery.

Meanwhile in 1888 William Crabtree had come of age, and he and his cousin David Crabtree became equal partners in the business. During the following 33

*Top: The main Machining Department in 1940. **Above left:** A Pattern Maker at work. **Left:** William Arthur Crabtree.*

years their partnership prospered.

By 1900 the monthly wage bill had risen to over £6,000 - a forty-fold increase during half a century, and in 1904 it was decided to buy an adjacent plot of land for expansion

The decision in 1921 to abandon the original weaving loom manufacture was a turning point in the firm's history. That same year also saw the beginnings of what would become the Metal Box Company, when four firms in the tin box and printing trades joined to form Allied Tin Box Makers Ltd, a name which was changed the following year to Metal Box and Printing Industries Ltd and subsequently, in 1930, to the Metal Box Company Ltd.

The firms which came together were similar to Lee & Crabtree – family businesses with years of experience and a long tradition in their trades. A new era of rapid expansion in the can making industry was about to begin, and as a manufacturer of the equipment used by the industry Lee & Crabtree was destined to grow with it during the following years.

In 1930 William Crabtree agreed to sell the business to the Metal Box Company and so became the first director of the newly constituted Lee & Crabtree Ltd.

Between 1931 and 1952 the number of employees rose from 97 to 435; sales rose from £22,000 to over £314,000 and floor space was more than doubled. Almost £190,000 worth of buildings and new plant was brought into use during those 21 years. The main building programme was begun in 1937 when new drawing offices, an office block, and fitting shop were built. The following year the factory was further enlarged by the purchase of premises known as Walker's Works, providing the firm with an additional 15,000 square feet of productive floor space.

When war broke out in 1939 for the next five years the company was fully employed making plant and tools for an endless variety of military equipment, ranging from land mines to mess tins, and from sten gun magazines to jigs and fixtures for the Beaufighter and Spitfire.

In addition the company also ran a training school for the Ministry of Labour in which some 400 women were trained in the operation of all kinds of machine tools.

To meet the insatiable demand a new press tool shop of 6,000 square feet was built. A new canteen was built in 1941 to seat 300 people and Hopefield House was bought for use as a hostel for Metal Box employees from other branches who came to Shipley for training.

The growing identification of Lee & Crabtree with its parent company reached its logical conclusion when in 1944 Lee & Crabtree Ltd formally ended its existence for the purposes of merging its assets with the main concern.

Above: The main Assembly Department, constructed in 1943. Above right: Charging the Copula with raw materials in the Iron Foundry. Right: The press tool making department - the profile irregular grinder producing the all ground, irregular press tool components - installed in 1948.

Three years later William Crabtree died at the age of 80. A devout Christian and brilliant engineer, during his long life he had been responsible for many patented improvements to weaving looms and sheet metal working machinery.

The post war years amply illustrated the value of the firm's machinery building capacity to the wider organisation, for without the resources at Shipley it would have been impossible to undertake the great programme of re-equipping which was necessary in order for the whole

business to take full advantage of new opportunities emerging.

Since the time that Lee & Crabtree had begun making sheet metal working machinery in 1887 the metal container and packaging industries had undergone revolutionary changes.

The development of the processed food can and the rapid growth of the canning industry all over the world depended upon the invention and production of high-speed machines capable of producing cans at a rate of more than 300 cans a minute.

In canneries too the process of filling and closing cans was becoming faster and faster.

If Metal Box was to prosper it was essential that the company should keep at the forefront of new developments, and that it should be able to equip and supply its own factories and supply customers with equipment of the highest standards.

Some of the spectacular growth of the Open Top can side of the business can be gained from the following figures: in 1930 some 23 million cans were made by Metal Box; in 1939 the figure was 636 million and by 1953 that number had risen to 1,300 million – a hundred cans a year for very household in the country.

Great developments had also taken place on the other side of the business where body makers from Shipley helped to equip Metal Box's General Line factories and thus supply British industry with containers for an endless range of products from baby powder to tennis balls.

Expansion of this scale reflected a considerable programme of investment in factory and plant. Following the war the greater part of the productive capacity and engineering skill at Lee & Crabtree had been employed to furnish the new Open Top can factories built by Metal Box to server canners in the United Kingdom and overseas. Closing machines too of many kinds were delivered to customers throughout the world. Presses ranging in size from the great 250 ton press especially built for the motor car industry to the smaller presses in use throughout Metal Box figure prominently in Lee & Crabtree's production records.

As Metal Box expanded overseas in Africa, India, and Pakistan, in Malaya and the West Indies so the market for machines built in Shipley expanded. The overseas market was not limited to those countries in which Metal Box operated. By the early 1950s the countries to which equipment was being sent from Shipley included Canada, Argentina, Sweden and Holland as well as many other parts of the Commonwealth, and penetration of the 'Dollar Markets'.

Equipment made in Shipley was not exclusively for tin box-making, MetalBox's investment in research and development bore fruit, new markets and new products were developed. The Shipley factory was frequently asked to design and build special machine tools to meet particular needs.

The building of machine tools for making bobbins for the textile industry was a good example of this kind of post war development; where once again 'Lee & Crabtree' re-established a connection with the industry which the firm's founders set out to serve more than a century earlier.

There was also an active social life at the factory in those days, centred on the sports hut which contained facilities for billiards, table tennis, darts and dominoes whilst the new canteen featured and excellent stage much used by the factory Dramatic Society.

In the late 1950s Metal Box decided that the Wrose Brow site was too small for its operations and bought the present site on Dockfield Road from the Bradford Council.

Work began in February 1962, and the first members of staff moved on site 12 months later, though it would take several years to be completed, including the foundry and final assembly bays.

The official opening in June 1966 was performed by Lord Kings Norton, the

Chairman of Metal Box. One of the official guests was Chairman of Shipley Council Councillor Jack King who was also an employee of Metal Box working in the factory, one of the 600 engineers or so who were employed on the site.

In the 1970s the technology for can-making changed significantly with the introduction of the two-piece can that is still used today for soft drinks, beer and some high volume foods. Shipley started to produce machines for that new can.

*Above right: A Jig Borer in the Press Tool Making Department. **Above right inset:** The company's M276 Double Wheel Tester finished in 1952. **Right:** The newly completed factory in 1970.*

By then the Shipley operation had become known as Metal Box Engineering, but in 1986 the parent company Metal Box merged with a French company to become CarnaudMetal Box.

Then in 1996 the US packaging group Crown Cork and Seal, now known as Crown Holdings, acquired the parent company. The Shipley operation however retains its name as CarnaudMetal Box Engineering.

Crown Holdings is a $7 billion metal packaging company with CarnaudMetalBox Engineering as the only company in the Crown family making machines.

In 1986 the business was awarded the Queen's Award for Technology for its development of technology to spin a shaped neck onto a two-piece can, a process which has been used throughout the world.

In common with many engineering companies the number of employees has reduced significantly, but 250 are still employed. In the last 30 years the business has increasingly spread its wings and now deals with more locations worldwide than ever before. The firm dispatches equipment as well as sales and technical staff to customers in 400 locations spread over 50 countries. Equipment is supplied to every major can-maker on every continent – testimony to the quality of engineering is that the firm is still providing spare parts for machines produced in Shipley over 50 years ago. The major product today is the two-piece can-maker which produces can bodies at the rate of 400 every minute.

The company operates in a very specialised market with only one other supplier in the world currently making similar products. It remains successful through the high level of technical expertise and support it provides to customers together with innovative products. Cans remain the most trusted of packaging options, with billions of cans for beverages, food, aerosols and many other purposes being produced every year. Now 'bottle cans' are appearing which are another aspect of the innovative nature of the can industry.

It will be a rare week when a reader of this book does not handle a can that has been made using a machine made in Shipley.

Top: Carnaud's assembly area, 2006. **Above:** *The 5000 Series Bodymaker, an advanced, horizontal, double action press for production of steel or aluminium DWI cans at high speeds and efficiencies (left) and the 5500 Canmaker, a new concept in 2-piece canmaking, based on the 5000 Series Bodymaker integrated with a new trimming unit (right).*

Joseph A Hey - A Fitting Farewell

There are only two certainties: death and taxes. We might be able to avoid taxes but no one avoids life's last act.

The passing of a loved one can present many problems, but with the professional help of an experienced Funeral Director many of those difficulties can be met and resolved with complete confidence in the outcome.

Joseph A. Hey & Son Ltd in Great Horton Road are Funeral Directors and Monumental Masons. The firm was established in Bradford in 1908. Today the Company is still an independent family owned and managed business. Joan (Jo) Hey Morphet holds a Diploma in Funeral Directing. She is part of the fourth generation of the family working in the firm and is the Company Secretary and Director. The company's business interests now extend to Monumental Masonry, with two separate companies importing directly from the country of origin and the development supply of innovative award winning environmentally friendly coffins and caskets. In 1990 Robert Morphet was appointed Managing Director of Joseph A. Hey & Son Ltd., he has worked in the funeral profession since leaving school in 1980. He holds a Diploma in Funeral Directing, a Diploma in Management Studies and a member of the British Institute of Embalmers. In 1997 he was awarded a Masters degree in Business Administration (MBA).

At the turn of the century it was quite unusual for men to change their occupations. The Victorian world was settled and prosperous in a way that seems astonishing

Top left: Mr & Mrs Joseph A Hey pictured towards the end of the 18th Century. Below: Herbert Hey circa 1925 standing alongside what is believed to be their first motor hearse. Top right: Herbert (left) alongside the company's special Stagecoach. Right: The Company's first motorised fleet of cars parked outside the garage entrance of 468-470 Great Horton Road in 1925, the site of today's premises.

sorter responsible for grading the daily intake of unwashed wool which arrived in the family owned mill at the junction of Thornton Road and City Road. Here he sorted the wool from hill and lowland sheep from home and the Antipodes according to its quality and the end product as carpeting or fine worsteds and broadcloth or for long lasting tweeds and serges.

When he was free from the demands of the mill he plied for hire, with a horse drawn four wheeler cab, such as a Brougham, borrowed from his undertaker father-in-law, outside the railway stations. This part time work was so successful that he bought two cabs of his own until, encouraged by his wife, he progressed, in 1908, to running an undertakers to cater for the post-Victorian way of death, still practised in the early years of the 20th Century. This was a natural step for a man who had married into the Manningham Lane undertaking family of Turnpenny of the firm Turnpenny and Coxon.

Bradford at the turn of the century was far removed from the unhealthily dangerous place it had been in the first four decades of the 19th Century though death was still a common visitor to the homes of families in all stations of life. Clean water was more readily available, especially in newer houses and sewage disposal was much better organised while medical science had made

to people accustomed to the uncertainties of the last decade or so. According to the contemporary hymn, All Things Bright and Beautiful, which ran 'The rich man in his castle, the poor man at his gate.... God ordered their estate.' Men tended to follow their father's profession or trade and literally stepped into his shoes, or rather his business or job, when he died. It was a simple solution, as old as time, to the complexities of making a living. Many traditional crafts were still practised in spite of the enormous advances made by new industries and the inventions which fostered them.

One of the adventurous innovators who made the nineteenth century such a rich and expansive era in British history was Joseph Arthur Hey. In the Belle Epoque of the Gay Nineties he was working as a wool

considerable advances during the Queen's long reign. Child death, however, was still frequent and consumption or tuberculosis was then incurable. The great outbreaks of King Cholera were past but infections and diseases which we can cure today were out and out killers still. Social conditions being what they were those whose diet and accommodation were sub-standard died more frequently than others more fortunately placed.

Meeting the regular cost of funerals was something for which many families saved with weekly payments to their local friendly societies in order to avoid the shame of having one's beloved buried in a pauper's grave. It is from these single purpose friendly societies that many of today's mighty insurance companies and building societies have grown.

Joseph Hey was built to be an undertaker as he was a tall imposing man who added an aura of his own to the black business uniform of Victorian England of knee length frock coat and a silk top hat. His life long love of music enabled him to conduct his business with the desired regularity of organisation, dignity and sympathetic bearing which were balm to his bereaved customers. In his spare time he participated in the tuneful activities of the Little Horton Orpheous Glee Union both as a member and as president.

With a desire to uphold, or better, the standards of his father-in-law's company Joseph Hey, aided by his knowledgeable wife, practised his profession with all the pride of one who does a job well. His brochures declared a policy of keeping abreast of the times and what exciting times the early decades of the new century were now that the old Queen was dead and fashions and customs were changing in the modern world!

The Hey family made available every possible facility to ease the troubles of those left behind by making the last journey of the deceased loved one as dignified and memorable as could be afforded.

Those same high standards are maintained by the present family business, following in the traditions adhered to by Joseph's son, Herbert, and daughters, Florence Emily (Emmie) and Sarahannah who developed the company in the second generation. It was their generation who took the revolutionary step of replacing horse drawn hearses with motor cars in the 1920s, although horses were still kept for a time, for those who preferred the sheer magnificence of shiny black horses bedecked with sable feathers.

A Private Service Chapel was installed in 1930 next to a dignified Reception Room where mourners could meet without being stared at. Such a facility was then unique

FUNERAL OF MR. R. HANNAM.

There was a large gathering of mourners at the funeral at Undercliffe Cemetery, Bradford, yesterday, of Mr. R. J. Hannam, a well-known Bradford sportsman, and at one time a prominent racehorse and greyhound owner.

The service was conducted by the Rev. G. E. N. Molesworth, Vicar of All Saints'.

Among the many personal friends were Messrs. W. Alderson, J. J. Bean, T. P. Petherbridge, H. C. Virr, T. Holland, J. L. Margerison (Menston), C. Gautier, W. Dixon, — Tordoff, A. Kelly (Harrogate), G. R. Wood (Bradford), John Carr (Heckmondwike), C. H. Lord (Bradford), R. Baxter and M. Hogg (Stocks Brewery), Isaac Neaton, Albert Cowling, J. Macdonald, and R. Rothera. Mr. H. Walker represented Walker and Hannam, Ltd., of Bradford.

Messrs. Joseph A. Hey and Son were the undertakers.

and the thoughtfulness was much appreciated by those who found a funeral gathering in the public rooms of an hotel exacerbated their ordeal to an unbearable level. The famous department store, Brown & Muffs, ran their

Left: The funeral of a Mr R Hannam, 1928, a well-know Bradford sportsman and a one time greyhound and racehorse owner, notice the horse made from flowers on top of the hearse. ***Top:*** *Herbert (right) and Arthur (left) Hey receiving a new fleet of Austin Princess Limousines in 1965.* ***Above:*** *An early Joseph Hey & Son Rolls Royce hearse.*

own Funeral Director Services for the benefit of life long clients who had furnished their homes and dressed their families under their hospitable roofs. When Brown & Muffs closed its funeral department the tasteful fittings were purchased by Hey & Son.

By the time Arthur Hey, the third generation of the Hey family, who had worked alongside his father for many years took over, the firm was one of the largest Funeral Directors in Yorkshire. Arthur went on to inherit and keep up the family's well-deserved reputation for service and dignity so important to those left behind. In the 1950s he bought the vacant premises at 468 and 470 Great Horton Road next to the existing premises which still contained the former stables. The entire block was redeveloped to provide under one roof the in-house facilities of joiners shop where coffins are made, a mortuary and sufficient garaging for a fleet of vehicles. The existing chapel was kept while the comfortable reception room was enlarged and the rest rooms established.

Today the chapel continues to provide a peaceful sanctuary in which a memorial service may be conducted. Hey's also provide quiet, dignified Rest Rooms where loved ones who have been removed from homes or hospitals in advance of the funeral arrangements can lie undisturbed from the hustle of modern life. These simple tasteful rooms enable relatives and friends to commune with and pray for, the dead in total privacy.

Hey's is proud of its staff, not least of those who, as registered members of the British Institute of Embalmers, prepare bodies for their farewell and final journeys.

The visit to see a loved one can bring considerable relief to a mourner who sees their relative totally relaxed and at peace. It is a biological fact that the skin of the deceased loses the marks of age and pain and the relative sees their loved one freed from all the worries or illness which may have marked their last years.

Hey family members still involved with the company are Joan (Jo) Hey Morphet, the Company Secretary, and Kathryn Hey. The company offers a funeral service second to none, even providing horse drawn hearses on request! Apart from the latter and the continuing quality and dignity, the modern funeral would appear very simple to the founders, accustomed as they were to the

flamboyance of their times. As costs of personal services have risen Hey's has marched with the times in offering pre-paid installment plans. As dealing with a death in the family is complicated enough by the legal and official matters Hey's also help to reduce the worries by offering an all-in service which can include funeral teas to replace the traditional Wake in the family home.

In May 2004 the company developed and submitted a Patent Application on a remarkable award-winning economic and eco-friendly alternative to the traditional coffin. The dictionary describes a coffin as a 'box in which a corpse is buried or cremated'. For anyone who needs to purchase one, a coffin is an emotional symbol of a close relative now-deceased.

For some families a coffin represents 'the way someone lived their life'; it might be the best that money can buy, or a very simple coffin. But for many others the coffin is only a necessary and unavoidable purchase that merely performs a practical function and 'it does not matter what it was made from if it's going to be cremated'. This point of view may also reflect the expressed wish of a relative before they passed away.

Top: Joseph A Hey & Son Ltd's Book of Remembrance. *Below:* The Private Chapel. *Right:* The Reception Room where relatives and friends meet prior to a service.

them with several original designs to provide a solution to current environmental, social and financial concerns a family may have when faced with making funeral arrangements.

Following on from the success of the Coffin Cover the company continued to innovate and develop the 'Honeycomb Coffin' and in May 2007 a further Patent Application was submitted. The Honeycomb range is now clearly established and look from the outside just like any other traditional burial or cremation coffin; what makes them unique is their construction. Instead of using Chipboard or MDF as the base material for the coffin, the Honeycomb casket is formed using over 90% recycled cardboard and paper that provides very strong, lightweight and environmentally friendly shell on which natural wooden veneers can be applied in the traditional way.

The Coffin Cover arrangement is a new and unique innovation in coffin design that combines all the necessary requirements of the traditional coffin with an enhanced visual appearance.

What makes the Coffin Cover arrangement different is that it contains a separate internal coffin that is made of a simple biodegradable material that is removed from the outer Coffin Cover prior to the cremation or the burial taking place.

But whatever clients' wishes, the firm and its staff are there to help. In an era when many family undertakers have sold out to large companies there remains a very welcome place for the personal touch that comes from a privately run business such as Joseph A Hey and Son Ltd, member of the National Association of Funeral Directors.

The simple and practical internal coffin is the only item that a family needs to purchase for the funeral because the outer Coffin Cover can be used again and again. The internal coffin is very low cost to produce and the savings are passed on to the family.

The Coffin Cover arrangement was developed using the best of all existing coffin features and combines

Top: Joan (Jo) Hey Morphet and husband Robert Morphet with a Coffin Cover and the environmentally friendly coffin from inside. Centre: A selection from the 'Honeycomb range' of coffins and caskets each made entirely of recycled paper and cardboard to make a strong lightweight environmentally friendly shell on which natural veneers can be attached. Right: Today's premises, comprising a complete funeral service under one roof. The Private Chapel entrance is seen on the far right of the picture.

Bulmer & Lumb - A Great Yarn

In 1931 Bulmer & Lumb Ltd was a new name in the established worsted spinning industry. Its origins lay in the Smith Bulmer Company, managed by Sir William Bulmer, which was based at Holmfield, Halifax. A dyehouse was opened there in 1920 to enable the company to concentrate on spinning coloured yarns. It was there in 1926 that JH Oates first met RJ Kennedy, men who would subsequently both become managing directors of Bulmer and Lumb.

These two men rejoined Sir William Bulmer in 1932. The previous year Sir William had formed Bulmer and Lumb, in partnership with Rowland Lumb to spin coloured worsted yarns at Prospect Mills, Wibsey. The firm continued to expand, and in 1937 became a public company.

In 1937 JH Oates took over from Sir William as Managing Director, a position he held until retiring with poor health in 1958. RJ Kennedy who had been assistant MD then managed the company until the mid-sixties, when the son of the original Sir William, also called William, took over the stewardship.

Sir William had opened a dyehouse (Prospect Dyeing Co.) at Bowling Mills soon after starting the spinning mill at Wibsey, and he brought in as manager Louis Stott who had originally managed the Holmfield Dyehouse.

Louis Stott had spent some time after his apprenticeship in Germany, which was

Above: Founder, Sir William Bulmer.
Right: JH Oates Managing Director from 1937 to 1958.
Below: Joseph Lumb and Sons Dyehouse, 1932/33.

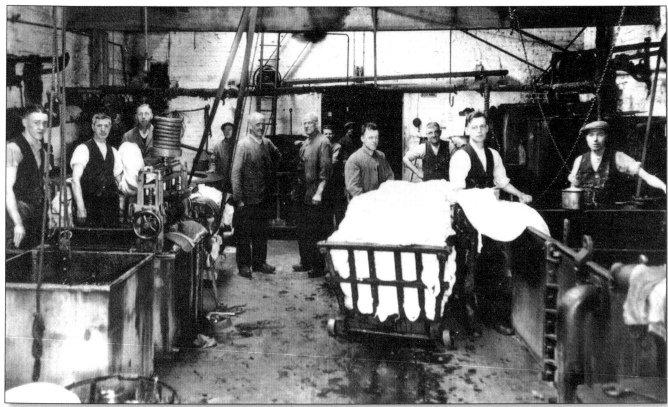

ranked high above all other countries for dyeware production, but had to return to the United Kingdom on the outbreak of the first world war. He remained dyehouse manager at PDC until the early 1950s.

Throughout the 1930s and 1940s Bulmer and Lumb acquired an excellent reputation for coloured yarns. During these years, as demand increased, the company bought several other factories, these being Oates Bros in Halifax, Walshaw Drake and Co in Brighouse, the Smith Heywood Group encompassing Blackburn and Sutcliffe and Joseph Sykes Recombers at Triangle, Bankfoot Mills, Victoria Mills in Eccleshill, and Providence Mills in Cleckheaton. The firm also rented property at Cumberland Works, Cemetery Road

Bradford as its central warehouse, and Montserrat Mills in Dudley Hill for warping.

Trading off its knowledge of top dyeing, the company was encouraged to start dyeing coloured tops for other spinners at home and abroad. The rather diverse sprawl of sites throughout the Bradford district gave rise to the need to consider new premises to centralise this still growing business. JH Oates had been impressed with the move accomplished by Patons and Baldwin from an old Victorian multi-storey set-up in Halifax to a purpose-built single-storey factory in Darlington just after the war.

By 1954 the site for a new mill had been researched and land was subsequently purchased at Buttershaw, some two miles away from the HQ at Wibsey. This 42 acre site, known as Royds Hall, had previously been occupied by a manor house, and two drift coal mines in an area dotted with similar mines from the 18th and 19th centuries.

The next two years saw the completion of planning and test boring (to check that previous site activities would not undermine the new structures). The new building took four

Top: Bulmer & Lumb directors and managers set off to Germany to study the latest machinery and working practices, 1950s. Above left: Operative training at B&L.

years from 1957 to 1961 to complete, putting up with problems like 70 days lost in 1958 due to an extraordinarily wet summer, and a trade recession which the board of directors decided was sufficient to halt building, but then quickly rescinded it.

In late 1959 the transfer of some dyeing equipment from Bowling Mills took place and was installed alongside the new Longclose pressure dye vessels. Dyeing started at Buttershaw in 1960. Also in the Bowling Tide Holidays of that year, the colour office was opened on the top floor. This was purpose-built to have northern daylight only, and had a staff of 16 colour matchers plus around 25 ancillary staff.

This first stage of the factory had required the removal of 60,000 tons of earth, 8,000 tons of rocks, and used 1,350 tons of steel, 12,000 tons of concrete, approx 1.25 million bricks, plus an unrecorded amount of dressed Yorkshire stone in the construction of this 180,000 square foot building. This was to reach 275,000 square feet when the second stage building was added in 1971/2.

At this stage the company employed over 1,400 people

in its Bradford area factories. The capacity for dyed tops had been 100,000 lbs per week from the old dyehouse facility but now the potential was more than doubled at Buttershaw. At its peak in the late 1960s and 1970s coloured top production reached 140 tons per week.

The main business of Bulmer and Lumb up to the opening of the Buttershaw mill was supplying pure wool and blends, suitable for weaving either as yarn or tops. The main qualities were wool from crossbreds through to merinos of no more than 19 micron fineness, wool/synthetic blends and wool/mohair. It is to the credit of the team that had evolved from the mid-1950s, that when approached by ICI with the fibre polyester it had invented and given the trade name 'Terylene', it was they who pioneered the successful dyeing and blending of this new fibre with wool, the main blend of 45/55 being a mainstay of Bulmer and Lumb to this day. The big change in processing synthetic/wool blends was the swing from using Noble combs, which

Top: An early staff outing.
Left: Another good day's work complete at Bulmer & Lumb Wibsey.

took out around 3-4% waste in the form of noil, over to the rectilinear comb (French comb) in the early 1970s which took out only around 1% noil with equal or better sliver cleanliness, this is important to the production of worsted yarn with good regularity and lack of faults.

The business was, and still is, more directed towards menswear final products, ranging from uniforms and corporate wear, through knitwear and hosiery to upholstery products. With the knowledge gained from the 1930s and 1940s in supplying major War Department contracts, the unsurpassed ability of the dyers and colour matchers at Bulmer and Lumb to produce large bulk lots which were homogenous for evenness of colour, coupled with "mirror" match repeatability was second to none.

Multiple retailers, notably M&S, were now able to mass-produce suits in a range of sizes for jackets and trousers 'off the peg'. This changed the whole menswear experience from that of going to the tailors, choosing a cloth, getting measured, coming back two or three weeks later for a fitting, then receiving the suit after five weeks, to that of an instant purchase. The 'suiting' business boomed from the early 1970s, with a major spinner of such cloth being John Haggas Ltd of Keighley, frequently in lots of 20 and 30 tons per colour, with Bulmer and Lumb supplying the dyed tops in lot sizes of up to 15 tons each (the spinner could blend lots in their drawing process, making spun lots up to 50 tons where required).

With the opening of the new dyehouse in 1960 and with the possibility of much higher production rates than previously, the board looked at hosiery spinning as a way to further expand operations, coupled with a move into 'dry' spinning (the traditional British system had always been to use oil-combed tops).

The number of employees in the B & L new group briefly exceeded 2,000 in 1964/65 after the company acquired the Bolton Eagle Ltd spinning group in 1964. This was essentially a singles yarn operation with deliveries often being made on spinning cop for customers to wind and clear before using. The group had several units (five spinning, one carpet and five knitting) dotted around the country from Leicester to Scotland, but many were not viable and a quick program of rationalisation saw the sell-off and closure of all but the core mill at Bolton.

By 1970 plans had been drawn up to extend the building at Buttershaw to accommodate the

Top: The Colour Office in 1961.
Left: Operating a Noble Comb in the Training Room, Wibsey. Early 1960s.

re-combing department and the entire spinning mills and warping and warehousing mills left in the district. Building the single-storey addition went very smoothly throughout 1971, and by 1972 the entire spinning operation of Bulmer and Lumb was being carried out from the Buttershaw and Bolton sites.

Production peaked in 1977/78 with dyed top production at 145 tons per week from Buttershaw, 75 tons per week from Walshaw Drake & Co in Brighouse and around 90 tons per week of loose stock dyeing from Blackburn and Sutcliffe at Triangle. Spinning production hitting 125 tons per week.

In 1977 one of the industry's largest orders was taken by HFH Hartley (ATC Group). Edward Wilson, its sales director, had pulled off a tremendous coup by selling 2.2 million metres of cloth to the Shah of Iran's military as 'civvies'. This resulted in a spinning order of some 990 tons being placed with John Haggas Ltd. The dyed tops were placed with Bulmer and Lumb. The same week that this order was booked at B & L there was another 350 tons of dyed top business placed from other customers. That one week of order bookings ensured maximum overtime for at least the next 18 months!

By the time the 1980s arrived however, the Buttershaw spinning plant was looking less and less viable as much of it was oil spinning machinery, both slower and of lesser quality than a modern dry spinning plant. Events then took a very definite turn as a serious fire at the Bolton factory meant that that factory required refurbishment under the terms of the insurance policy. This left the Buttershaw spinning plant totally out of date, not least as the best of the Bradford machines were shipped to Bolton to get that mill quickly back into production. By 1985 the three spans of the newest part of the building were empty. A short term fix of

Top: Bulmer & Lumb old factories: Harold Walker & Co. Eccleshill (top left), Oates Brothers Ltd, Halifax (top right), Bulmer & Lumb Ltd's Prospect Dyeing Co, Bowling (bottom left) and Prospect Mills, Wibsey (bottom right). **Above:** *W.P. Bulmer (later Sir William Bulmer) welcomes Miss World, Ann Sydney, on her visit to Bulmer & Lumb in 1964.* **Below:** *The newly completed Buttershaw site, 1961.*

The new millennium would see a major change in Bulmer & Lumb's organisation. In 2001 the management team bought out most of the wool worsted interests owned by ATC, and in January 2002 a new company called The Bulmer and Lumb Group Ltd was born. This is centred on the site at Buttershaw, but with the addition of the weaving business of HF Hartley (transferred from Wilsden), some space dyeing of hand knitting yarns, and the carding and scouring of synthetic fibres on commission for a customer making high-quality filters and medical masks.

During the following year the company acquired the weaving business of Arthur Harrison and in 2005 the highly regarded Taylor and Lodge Company of Huddersfield was added to the Group. The Huddersfield site being retained, it has also become home to the Arthur Harrison business.

installing a carpet yarn bulking unit, having made losses over two years, was also closed down. This section having been empty for a few months, it was decided that selling off that part of the building was the best solution: in 1986 it was sold, with several acres of the land to Yorkshire Water, eventually becoming its head office.

In late 1986 an offer to purchase the whole of the Bulmer and Lumb Group, by Allied Textile Companies, was accepted by the board. For the next 15 years the Bulmer and Lumb Group traded as a branch of Allied Textiles PLC. In 1988 the Bolton Eagle spinning plant was sold off by ATC as a management buyout. Three years later soaring interest rates made this venture unviable and the business closed down. Today Bolton Eagle mill is part of Bolton College of Technology.

By 1987 ATC had installed a yarn package dyeing unit (ATC Dyers) alongside the top-dyeing machines at Buttershaw. This was previously located at Joseph Lumb's site in Huddersfield. Recently the package dyeing plant has been increased in size from a 7 ton a week plant to 20 tons plus.

The synthetic topmaking arm of the Sir James Hill Group was purchased by ATC in 1991 and managed by the B & L team. In 1996, after 5 years based in Keighley, an extension was added at Buttershaw to house this 'white' operation.

Meanwhile, in 1993, ATC bought the spinning mill of John Foster at Queensbury. The B & L team managed this site as part of the B&L operation within ATC. Some £3m was soon invested in new equipment there besides installing the best of the machinery from Scarboro' Mills in Halifax (trading as Willey and Pearson).

In 2006 space was allocated at Buttershaw to allow Harrison Gardner of Liversedge to restructure its hank dyeing and space dyeing operations there. This operation is still run by the Harrison family independently of Bulmer & Lumb.

Today the B & L Group remains one of the UK's leading textile companies employing 280 people over its two sites.

*Top: The Spinning Department, 1972. **Below:** An aerial view of Bulmer & Lumb, Buttershaw, 2007.*

Don Whitley Scientific - The Centre of Science in Shipley

Did you hear about the prestigious Shipley firm that's been exporting rabbits to Kazakhstan? If you did then there is nothing wrong with your hearing – but you'd be under a serious misapprehension in imagining that the 'rabbits' in question had fur and a fondness for lettuce. The RABIT, as it is actually called, is an innovative piece of equipment for use in microbiological laboratories. The Kazakhstan Ministry of Health recently purchased fourteen units.

Today Don Whitley Scientific Limited is a renowned business, based in Otley Road, Shipley. The company develops, manufactures and sells instrumentation and associated products for microbiological applications worldwide. In addition it provides microbiological contract services in DEFRA registered and GLP-compliant laboratories. It sells to both private and public sectors in a variety of scientific disciplines, and supports its products throughout the world through a carefully chosen distributor network.

The company's wealth of experience in microbiology, product development and engineering has led to the design and manufacture of a range of innovative equipment specified by leading scientists throughout the world. Brand names recognised by all in the field include the MACS range of workstations, the WASP Spiral Plater and RABIT (Rapid Automated Bacterial Impedance Technique).

Products and services are sold in more than 40 countries. These range from simple reagents to automated instrumentation for the detection and enumeration of micro-organisms.

For over 30 years Don Whitley Scientific has deservedly been garnering business and professional accolades. The story of how the company came into being is a remarkable one; it is a story which involves both inspiration and perspiration – both, according to Thomas Edison, the essential ingredients of genius. It is also a story which records triumph over adversity, and a never say die determination to

Above: *Founder Don Whitley pictured with a Darlington Glass Rose Bowl presented to him by the Society of Anaerobic Microbiology for his contribution to anaerobic microbiology.* ***Below left:*** *Anaerobic jars and accessories.* ***Below:*** *Where it all began, Don Whitley's house in Shipley in the mid 1970s.*

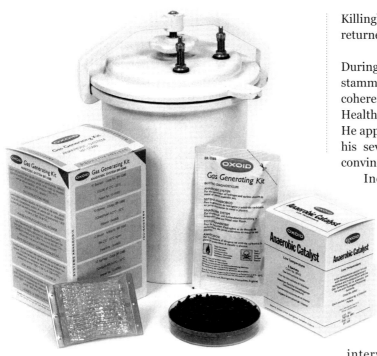

Killingbeck Hospital when it was a TB Sanatorium and then returned to the Leeds Maternity Hospital as Chief MLSO.

During these years, Don battled to overcome a severe stammer, which, at times left him almost incapable of coherent speech. Don decided that he wanted to leave the Health Service and begin a career in the commercial world. He applied for eighteen jobs as a medical representative but his severe speech impediment did nothing to help him convince interview panels that he was the man for the job. Indeed, he was openly laughed at during some interviews as his speech deteriorated when he felt under stress.

It was after one such interview that Don, by way of consolation, treated himself to fish and chips wrapped in the time-honoured way in newspaper. As he screwed up the paper at the end of his meal he saw an advert for a Sales Representative for Oxoid Limited. He duly sent off an application and was called for interview. So sure that this interview would go the way of all the others and that he would not get the job, he relaxed, did not stammer, sold himself well and the position was his!

Top left: One of the company's early anaerobic jars and gas generating kits. ***Below:*** *The Don Whitley Model D Spiral Plater, considered at the time to be an essential item of laboratory equipment.*

succeed whatever obstacles might be in the way. It is of course the story of the company founder, Don Whitley himself.

Born in London in 1929, the elder son of a fitter with J Lyons and Co, Don, along with his family, escaped the war-torn capital when decentralisation of the Lyons tea packing operation meant relocation to Leeds. Don was educated at Morley Grammar School, where he fostered an ambition to study medicine. His parents however were of the opinion that being a doctor was 'not for the likes of us' and he was rapidly dissuaded from taking such a career path.

On leaving school Don became an assistant in the textile research department at Leeds University, a job he hated. It was there that he avidly read copies of 'The Lancet' and would see advertisements for medical laboratory assistants. Don wrote to twenty-two Leeds hospitals and nursing homes in the hope of finding such a job. As luck would have it, the matron at The Women's Hospital in Leeds passed his letter on to its laboratory that was indeed looking for a trainee technician. It was whilst working there that Don gained his Intermediate and Associateship in Microbiology and his Fellowship in Haematology. For many years he was the Secretary of the West Yorkshire Branch of what is now known as the Institute of Biomedical Sciences. Don was eventually made Chief Medical Laboratory Scientific Officer (MLSO) at

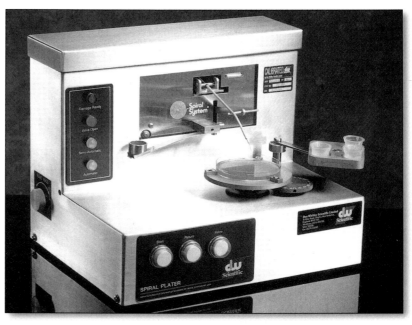

That was in 1956. Don worked very successfully in this role, building up business in his assigned area, while also establishing strong scientific and personal relationships with numerous post graduate students at Leeds University Medical School, many of whom went on to great achievements in microbiology.

Due to family ties, Don eschewed offers of promotion, which would have meant moving away from the North but eventually accepted a position with Becton Dickinson Ltd, promoting and selling BBL culture media. He left them after eighteen months to join the Bydand Group of companies, becoming the Sales Manager of RB Turner Ltd, then moving on to become Technical Manager of Stayne Veterinary Ltd where he helped develop a commercial kit for the screening of cattle for Brucellosis with the Rose Bengal Antigen. He eventually became Technical Director of the RB Turner Glass Division in Bishop Auckland which was producing blood collection tubes amongst other items. Shortly after this new appointment the Bydand Group sold out to Becton Dickinson and Don left the company.

During his time in the Health Service, Don had become friends with John Trowbridge, a microbiologist at the Royal Berkshire Hospital. Don took John with him, first to Becton Dickinson and then to the Bydand Group, culminating in John becoming Sales Manager for RB Turner when Don was Sales Director. Once Becton Dickinson had bought the company, Don and John decided to set up in business together. Their joint venture, LIP Services, was set up in Don's house in Shipley. The company sold culture media and plastic disposables. After three years, Don felt that his ambition lay in designing new products and he sold his 25% share to John for £5,000 and with this money, Don Whitley Scientific Limited (DWS) was born in 1976.

*Top: Don Whitley's RABIT - Rapid Automated Bacterial Impedance Technique. **Above:** WASP – Whitley Automated Spiral Plater. **Right:** The company's flexible, efficient, easy to use MK 3 Workstation with satellite, manufactured between 1985 and 1994.*

It was hardly an auspicious year to start a business: galloping inflation was running at over 25 per cent. The new Prime Minister Jim Callaghan, taking over from Harold Wilson, inherited an cconomy on the verge of collapse with an unprecedented number of strikes making Britain 'the sick man of Europe'.

Nevertheless that year the newly formed DWS placed an advert in a journal showing a photograph of a baby - Don's youngest child – sitting in an anaerobic jar. The caption on that advertisement read: From tiny acorns mighty oak trees grow. It was a startlingly accurate prediction.

Don designed a new anaerobic jar incorporating Schrader valves. These were also incorporated into the design of a new jar for Oxoid Limited which won a design award and is still manufactured today. The new jars swept the market allowing the tiny company to expand and be recognised in a highly competitive field.

Don then designed a hydrogen generating system, a carbon dioxide generating kit for growing microaerophillic bacteria such as *Campylobacter* spp -

and a low temperature palladium catalyst, still used today in anaerobic jars. Oxoid also took up these products.

In the late 1970s Don designed an anaerobic cabinet, the Mark 1, which revolutionised how laboratories isolated anaerobic bacteria. It had fewer leaks due to the method of construction, less condensation due to the external desiccant system and more catalyst allowing a lower oxygen concentration than apparently similar products on the market. DWS quickly became a leading player in the UK market, with the workstations being continuously developed through the Mark 2, WISE, Mark 3 and Compact models. The Mark 3 was the first workstation to incorporate a patented three-gas mixing system. DWS was also granted a patent for the development of Anotox™, an atmosphere scrubbing device that extends the life of catalyst in workstations. The company's current range of Modified Atmosphere Controlled Systems (MACS) are UK and world market leaders.

Don also introduced spiral plating to the UK from the United States. Dr Ed Campbell invented the process. His products were sold through an associated company, Spiral Systems Marketing, owned by Sam Schalkowsky. The

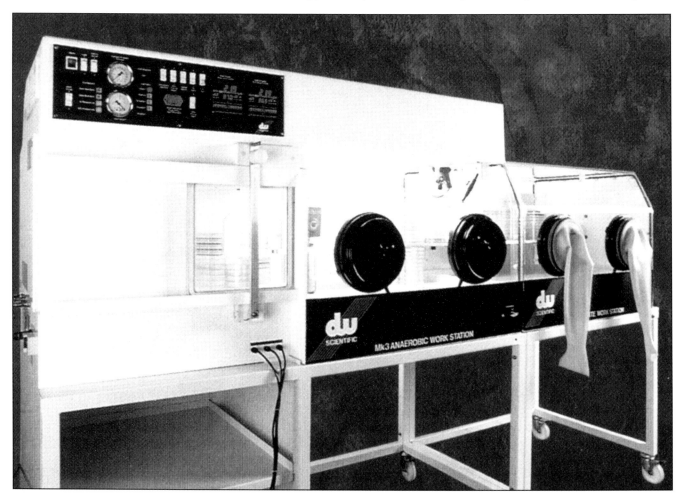

product was launched as the Model A Plater and progressed through a series of models.

In 1993, DWS launched its own spiral plater, WASP – the Whitley Automated Spiral Plater. WASP became a market leader.

It was Don who suggested the principles of gravimetric diluting whilst in a bar on the Florida Keys with Sam Schalkowsky. Spiral Systems went on to produce the first model and now a number of models exist. DWS sells versions manufactured by AES Laboratoire. Don was involved with the early commercial development of the Malthus impedance system produced by Torry Research in 1977. As DWS grew, it became possible for Don to look at producing his own system. Launched in 1987, Rapid Automated Bacterial Impedance Technique (RABIT) soon became a strong player in the market and is still an important product for the company both in the UK and overseas.

Since 1986 contract microbiology services have also been offered by the company. Contract research studies embrace all aspects of antimicrobial development programmes including efficacy, safety and clinical trial studies with increasing emphasis on antimicrobial resistance work. Laboratory staff also have extensive experience in working within the animal feed industry as well as with the medical device, textiles, food and chemical industries.

A diverse, international customer base includes quality assurance personnel, food producers, public sector microbiologists, clinical microbiologists and research and development specialists.

The company that Don founded in 1976 now owns smaller subsidiary companies in Germany and Australia. The emphasis on product development is still strong with more than 10% of turnover being spent in this area. The company has received numerous SMART and Spur awards in recognition of its outstanding product development record.

The company enjoys a wealth of experience in microbiology, design, engineering and marketing, skills amply demonstrated by Don Whitley Scientific's ability to design and manufacture a range of high quality and often ingenious equipment specified by scientists throughout the world. In recognition of these achievements the company received Millennium Product status for two products - the MACS range of anaerobic and variable atmosphere workstations, and the WASP spiral plater. Millennium Products were the UK national initiative to identify and promote innovation through new products and services created in Britain for the millennium. Millennium Products were selected because they were forward-thinking, challenging, creative and innovative.

Still based in Shipley, West Yorkshire, the company is now housed in 3,000 square metre premises on Otley Road. The science of microbiology is very important to the company and to Don; twelve microbiologists are employed in laboratory, sales and product support roles. Don Whitley's main achievement however will remain the way he is regarded in the industry. His business ideals of helping the customer wherever he can still survive in this family business that now incorporates three generations of his family.

In 1995, in recognition of his contribution to anaerobic microbiology, Don was made the First Honorary member of the Society for Anaerobic Microbiology. He is still regularly consulted on the development of new DWS products and continues to attend the meetings of various scientific organisations.

The story of Don Whitley and of the company he founded, Don Whitley Scientific, is truly inspirational. No doubt Don himself would modestly say he was lucky: others would say however that through relentless hard work, applied ambition and an absolute refusal to be cowed by adverse circumstances, Don beat all the odds and made his own luck.

In a fine tribute Paul Walton, Don's eldest son and now Managing Director of DWS, sums up his father's achievements in just a few words: 'There can be few microbiologists in the world who have not used something in which Don has had a hand'.

Top left: The well-equipped DEFRA registered and GLP-compliant DWS laboratories. Left: The MACS MG 500 Anaerobic Workstation. Below: Don Whitley Scientific's premises in Otley Road, Shipley.

To Market, to Market - Bradford Markets

Being taken to 'the market' as a child is one of those memories that linger forever. In many ways it makes little difference where that market actually was: what stays riveted in the mind is the bustle of the crowds, the smell of fresh oranges mingling with that of toffee and fish. Then there was the noise – the shouts of the greengrocers and butchers bellowing out the quality and cheapness of their wares, and in the indoor markets that slight echo which gives such places a very different 'feel' from the world outside.

The city of Bradford and its surrounding district are uniquely blessed with a number of markets, both indoor and outdoor. Across the generations, and across many centuries, local folk have taken their wares to market, and taken themselves and their children to sample what is the oldest form of retailing.

Bradford Council runs three indoor retail markets in addition to a wholesale market and three open markets.

The earliest town within the ambit of Bradford Council for which evidence exists of a market is the pleasant Wharfedale town of Ilkley nestling under the great mass of Rombalds Moor. The Romans came here and named it Olicana in the first century AD. They gazed at the ancient moorland stone carvings, as puzzled by them as we are today. The time span that separated them from the carvers is the same 2,000 years that separates us from the Romans. The Roman fort, like all Roman forts throughout

the Empire, attracted an adjacent market. Oddly enough, despite this early market, the town never gained an ancient Market Charter, spending its days as a rural backwater until he Victorians discovered the health-giving properties of its spa. Ilkley's golden days began with White Wells and the tourists who came there for 'the cure'. Today the spa and fort have left few traces, but the town still attracts tourists for its moor and riverside walks. The Council also runs two stalls on the central car park on the site of the Roman market. With its attractive shops, splendid scenery and genteel air Ilkley is a rewarding place to visit and shop.

Bingley lies on the main route between Keighley and Bradford overlooked by the dramatic rocky outcrop of Druids Altar which Disraeli used in his novel 'Sybil'. Bingley Market gained its Charter from 'Bad King' John of Robin Hood fame. In fact King John signed neither the local Market Charter nor the more famous Magna Carta, like all his Norman and Plantaganet predecessors on England's throne, he was illiterate. Bingley's thriving market has left traces of its later magnificent 18th century Market Hall and Medieval Butter Cross. A price list from 1720 – roughly contemporary with the Hall – survives, showing a pair of gloves costing eleven shillings (55p) whilst for ninepence (almost 4p) one could buy two chickens. In the 1880s the local Town Council bought the market rights from the successor to the feudal Lords. The town boasts an historic church with an Anglo-Saxon font carved with runes. The

Open Market is still put on by the Council, whilst an indoor market is held without Council involvement. Visitors are attracted by the quaint shops, and walks in the nearby St Ives estate, rich in bird life and squirrels.

Bradford itself boasts two markets in close proximity to one another. 'Brafford', as it then was named, received its Charter from Henry III in 1251. In a subsequent dispute with Bingley at the end of the 19th century Bingley was quick to point out that although Bradford's charter was issued by King Henry their own Charter was issued by Henry's father King John and thus had precedence.

The Bradford Charter went to Edmund de Lacy –a man with an Anglo-Saxon Christian name and a Norman surname. King Henry III was in residence at the old Anglo-Saxon battle site town of Merton when he appended his seal to the charter in April 1251. 'Know ye that we have granted and by this our present charter confirmed, to our beloved valet, Edmund de Lacy, that he and his heirs forever, shall have one market every week on Thursday at his manor of BRAFFORD, in the county of York, unless this market be to the injury of neighbouring markets.'

Top left: The old Butter Market. **Left and above:** *Views of Rawson Place Market's exterior and Butcher's Section, circa 1930.*

Today a flagstone commemorating this event can be seen outside the Oastler Shopping Centre entrance.

The charter's reference to the 'injury to neighbouring markets' also occurs in the Bingley charter granted by King John. This clause was designed to prevent the local Lord of the Manor infringing the market rights of his neighbouring fellow lord. The distance between one market and another was set out by Judge Bracton at a later date to be six and two-thirds miles. This distance was based on a man's ability to walk 20 miles a day, and allowed for the outward trip, time spent buying and selling and then the return walk home.

As with most ancient charter towns Bradford's charter was reissued and amended by later monarchs to suit prevailing tastes and circumstances.

Bradford received a second charter in 1294 when Edward I, Edward Longshanks, the 'Hammer of the Scots' and son of Henry III gave Henry de Lacy the right to hold an annual fair. This charter was enacted in June of that year from the palace of Westminster. The fair was eventually discontinued, but other new charters were issued to suit changing times

Despite the official market day of Thursday early markets tended to be held on Sundays near the church, and this is reflected in the name of Kirkgate Market. It is worth recalling the then very small population that the local markets had to cater for in those early days. In 1310 for example the population of Bradford was just 650. The markets were held at the side of the Parish Church,

now elevated into a Cathedral. It is said that the stump of Bradford's medieval market cross, which can now be seen in Kirkgate Market was created when an over-zealous Roundhead in the 1640s chopped off the cruciform section during the Civil War with the cry 'No pompe nor pride let God be honoured'. Mince pies at Christmas were also banned by Cromwell's Puritans on the alleged basis that they impiously represented Christ in the manger in the form of a sweetmeat. There was a cell under the Market Cross for imprisoning those who contravened Market Law.

The market had moved at some point to Westgate where it remained for some centuries, until in 1801 it moved further up the hill. New buildings fronted on to New Street which was then renamed Market Street, remaining so to this day. The new market site was however not a success.

In 1824 it moved again to area of the present Kirkgate Market. The buildings in Market Street would be demolished. These would be remembered in Bradford as the Butter Market. Miss Elizabeth Rawson , Lady of the Manor, in 1865 assigned her Market rights to Bradford Council on a 999-year lease for a payment of £5,000 per annum.

A new Kirkgate Market, itself to be demolished in 1973, was completed in 1878 and is still remembered with great affection by Bradfordians. The total cost of building was £83,381. The bottom half was opened in October 1872 and the top half in May 1878, the whole comprising an area of 7,404 square yards. Abutting on to Kirkgate, Darley Street and Godwin Street the market was open daily for the sale of miscellaneous goods including drapery, millinery, boots, shoes, hardware, toys, fancy goods, provisions, confectionery, refreshments, books, music and flowers. The building from an architectural point alone enabled it to rank as one of the finest market halls in the country at a time when towns and cities were vying with one another to build the most outstanding markets possible. Entering via a great arch it seems in hindsight to have been an Aladdin's cave with its columns, large semi-circular windows and a rich array of diverse items for sale. It contained 136 stalls and 52 shops. In those days it jostled with the public library for space which

occupied a considerable portion of the first and second floors of the exterior of the building.

The present Kirkgate Market was built at the side of the 19th century market and opened in 1973; the old market was then demolished: part of the Kirkgate Centre (formerly the Arndale Centre) now covers the site of the popular Victorian market.

A little way up the hill from Kirkgate stands the Oastler Market (formerly known as John Street Market). This site was acquired by the Council in 1920 from the Copy Quarry estate. Various pot fairs and pleasure fairs were held on the site until in 1929 a new market was built with open stalls and a glazed roof. This was a very advanced design for the time. In 1969 this market was demolished and the new John Street Market appeared with angled stalls not unlike the pre-decimal three-penny bits. Sadly the new market was not destined for a long life – in 1974 it

Top left: *James Street Market, shortly before being converted into a Fish Retail Market.*
Left and below: *Two early photographs of St James Market, the Wholesale Fruit Market (left) and Meat Market (below).*

burned down, apparently due to a cardigan having been left on a radiator. The following year the present market was built.

This market is the third on the site, and even the present one was modified greatly in 2002. It boasts an array of butchers and even some fishmongers (a trade hard to find these days). The rest of the market, like Kirkgate, has jewellers, cloths stalls, sweet and biscuits stalls and all the traditional run of market wares. It takes its name from Richard Oastler (1789-1861) who campaigned tirelessly for a better deal for child textile workers. His statue is at the side of the market. With two markets so close, and all manner of other shops around, this is a 'shopaholics heaven'.

Keighley Market sits in the town affectionately known as the 'Jewel of the Aire'. Near to Haworth and Bronte Country, Keighley boasts a steam railway from a station site used by the Bronte sisters. The town sits in the Aire Valley and Rombalds Moor spreads itself from Ilkey to brood over Keighley too.

In the middle of the town is one of the ancient cup and ring stones transported from the great moor

Right and below: *Pre-war shopping at the Kikgate Market.*

where it was carved about 4,000 years ago. Henry de Keighley obtained Keighley's market charter from Edward I in 1305 and a list of market prices from 1312 still survives: wheat was being sold for six shillings (30p) a quarter and eggs were a halfpenny a dozen. From 1833 to 1970 the market stood just below Church Green on what is now a small car park. From its

present site the tower of Keighley Parish Church can still be seen. The market has not moved far from its original site. A shopping day in Keighley can be supplemented by trips to 'Bonnie Cliffe Castle' (as the Keighley poet Bill 'th'Hoyus End called it) or to the historic East Riddlesden Hall with its Anglo-Saxon stone and ghostly legends.

The indoor market at Shipley is not Council-run, but the Outdoor Market is and stands in Market Square where the Victorian market stood. Shipley has no ancient charter, although like all the other market towns mentioned here it does feature in the Domesday Book of 1086. A pleasant sylvan idyll for most of the centuries, and chiefly noted as a place where monks grazed their sheep, Shipley only sprang to life as a busy little town in Victorian times. Well-placed on the Keighley to Bradford road and well served by public transport Shipley could be fitted comfortably as part of a trip to the area's other markets.

Lastly the only other market to mention is not central to any town, nor is it open to the public. This is the wholesale St James' Market at Essex Street in Bradford. This is a busy market active in the early hours. The original building was constructed in 1874; it once boasted four banks, a Post Office, a thriving railway station and a crane with a 20-ton lift.

The present building deals mainly with fruit and flowers and was built in 1976.

But do 'old fashioned' markets have any future? Aren't concrete shopping malls, national chains and huge super stores what the public want? Yes the public may want those things, but at the same time they equally appreciate buying from individual stallholders in a shopping environment on a human scale – a tradition that has local roots stretching back two thousand years. Whatever the future may bring, one thing we can be certain of – Bradford's markets are here to stay.

It is extremely heartening to know that the future of Bradford City Centre will have a Markets theme at its heart. One of the four neighbourhoods for the Rebirth of the City is to be built around a Markets theme. In addition, the plans for the Park in the Heart and Mirror Lake will see themed Market events take place in a world class City Centre for many years to come. Long live Markets!

Above and left: *The familiar sight of a bustling John Street Market.*

Bradford Markets would like to thank David Mosley for his work in researching this article.

Paying Attention to Bradford Grammar School

'Hoc Age' is the Latin motto of Bradford Grammar School. Literally it means 'Do this!' although a more free translation renders its meaning as 'Pay Attention!'. And certainly the school located on Keighley Road is an educational establishment well worth paying attention to.

Bradford Grammar School, today including the Junior School, Grammar School and Sixth Form, is a selective co-educational school which aims to retain the best of the traditional grammar school ethos with a modern, forward-thinking approach. Its objective is to achieve excellence in all it does: not only in academic matters, but also in the outstanding range of extra-curricular opportunities it offers, so giving young men and women the qualifications and the confidence they need to play a leading role in tomorrow's society.

The school has existed since about 1548 and was incorporated by royal charter in 1662. A mile from the centre of Bradford, it comprises five main buildings on a 20-acre site. These include the Clock House, a 17th-century manor house for the juniors and the handsome senior school (opened in 1949). More modern buildings house the library and IT centre, a sports hall and the Hockney Theatre. Most recently, a sixth form centre, music school, swimming pool and all-weather pitch have been completed. Its overall amenities are first-rate. It is in the process of becoming fully co-educational and over a third of pupils are now girls: girls have been admitted to the sixth form since 1984, and in all intakes from 1999. The two principles of discipline laid down are: firstly, that pupils are expected to know what is and what is not good conduct and to do nothing likely to bring themselves and their school into disrepute; secondly, that study is a discipline in itself. It provides a sound, traditional education in many branches of learning and sets very high all-round standards. It has long been one of the country's most distinguished schools and examination results are excellent. It enjoys strong local support. Sports and games are played to a very high standard with successful regional and national

Top: *Bradford Grammar School in Manor Row circa 1830.* ***Left:*** *A late 19th century view of the new School in Hallfield Road.*

representation (e.g. rugby, cross-country, netball, table tennis and tennis). There is a wide range of clubs and activities.

Exactly when the school began, however, is something of an historical mystery: its early records have long been lost. Certainly the school existed in the 16th century and other schools in the county were given Royal charters in 1548 in the reign of the boy king Edward VI. What is not in doubt is that, following the tumult of the Civil War, the Commonwealth and the Restoration, Charles II granted the school another Charter, still preserved at the school, a document which would remain the basis of its legal status until 1871.

The earliest school building was located in Church Bank.

Tiny by today's standards the school relocated to a far larger building in Manor Row in 1820. Even the new building was capable of accommodating just 120 pupils – yet remarkably it never held even half that number. By 1861 the school had just 56 pupils, yet six years later numbers had almost doubled, and by 1875 had risen to 415.

A major reorganisation and re-launch in 1871 had wholly reinvigorated the school and led to a move to Hallfield Road in 1872 – a building which would be home for the school for the next 76 years.

According to the Bradford Observer:

The new building is planned upon the 'Class-room', or as it is sometimes termed 'the Prussian system', which consists of a large hall for the purpose of assembly and a number of class-rooms in which is carried on the work of the schools. We may state that ordinary English schools consist almost entirely of one large schoolroom.

It was in this building that generations of Bradford boys received their education – not least such famous names as musician Frederick Delius who attended the school from 1874 to 1878, the

Left: An early twentieth century photograph of BGS staff. **Below:** *The Art Room in 1912.*

Astronomer Royal Sir Frank Dyson who was at the school from 1882 to 1886, and Sir Mortimer Wheeler, archaeologist, writer and broadcaster who was a pupil at Bradford Grammar School between 1899 and 1905.

Like all schools Bradford Grammar's old boys made their contribution and sacrifices in the Great War – the first world war as it would later be known. Around 1,150 of them served in the forces, 445 as officers. Over 200 paid the ultimate price for their patriotism. Poignantly Ernest Sichel an Old Boy of the school, but of German background, designed the school war memorial unveiled in 1920 and listing the 215 former scholars who would never return.

The interwar years were consumed by the urgent need to find new and better premises – and the funding to pay for them. As early as 1919 Clock House, a large 17th century house and its estate, was identified as a suitable location for a new school. The struggle to raise funds would go on for many years. Building work on a completely new school would not in fact begin until 1936 – almost on the eve of the second world war.

This page: HRH The Duke of Edinburgh unlocks the front door thereby opening the new School (pictured above), 1949.

Famous old boy Denis Healey – Lord Healey of Riddlesden – subsequently Chancellor of the Exchequer left in 1936 and did not see the new school completed; though others such as painter David Hockney RA would spend most of their schooldays at the new buildings, whilst Olympic Gold medal-winner the swimmer Adrian Moorhouse who attended the school from 1972 to 1982 would never know the old school building at all.

Nor would Lord Healey have experienced a curious wartime novelty – a female teacher! Remarkably, apart from teachers of 'Prep' there had been no female teacher at the school until 1941 – Margaret Baker would remain on the staff until 1958, continuing to be the sole female teacher. And there would be none after that until 1976.

Despite those critical reserves of building materials it was not until January 1949 that the new school building was officially opened – by no less a personage than HRH the Duke of Edinburgh.

The decades since 1949 have been ones of unprecedented peace and prosperity for Britain. In those decades thousands of pupils have passed through the doors of Bradford Grammar School.

All of those many students will have happy memories of the school and 'the best days of their lives'. Yet the years of peace have not been static. Though the underlying ethos of the school may be unalterable many other changes have taken place. Old Boys who were at the school thirty or forty years ago will note the introduction of a five day week in 1975 – Saturday morning school being consigned to the history books along with school caps and 'Houses'.

Teaching too has changed: science has triumphed over the classics, and today computers have replaced scouting. And of course the school is no longer solely restricted to boys.

As for the fabric of the school itself, though the building may have been completed in 1949 nothing stands still. Changes to the original school building and the creation of new blocks have ensured that Bradford Grammar School remains not simply fit for purpose but provides first-class facilities fit for education in the 21st century.

Today the school has over 1,000 pupils and more than 100 members of the teaching staff. Under Headmaster Stephen Davidson, in post since 1996, the school continues to ensure that young people are fully prepared to 'pay attention' to the future whilst looking back with pride to the past.

Work on the new school building progressed through the early part of the war, but during 1940, as the building neared completion, it was taken over by the army, first as a training barracks and then as a hospital. Happily fine wooden floors, panelling and much other building materials though on-site had not yet been installed – they were hidden away in the basement and the entrance bricked up for 'the duration'. Bradford Grammar School would miraculously be able to forge ahead with its building programme at the end of the war in 1945 despite the building materials shortages encountered by almost everyone else.

Meanwhile during the war pupils made their own contributions to the war effort: 100 worked on farms helping bring in the harvest living on farms for six weeks. Meanwhile the number of pupils had soared from 664 in 1939 to 925 in 1945 as the textile industry boomed due to wartime demands.

Top left: The former Jagger Library, circa 1949. Above left: Sixth Form Drama students in the annual autumn Showcase. Left: The Music School balcony over-looking the Sixth Form Centre.

H C Slingsby - Keeping Business Moving

The firm of HC Slingsby, today based in Otley Road, Baildon, has been a familiar name in the Bradford area for more than a century. In 1961 the company went public and became HC Slingsby plc. Several members of the Slingsby family remain on the board of directors, still driving the business forward in the 21st Century.

Today the company's catalogue of commercial and industrial equipment for the workplace runs to an incredible 1,345 pages. The twice-yearly publication lists over 30,000 products.

The Slingsby label can be found on the pallet trucks used in supermarkets where storeroom staff will be assisted by large warehouse steps. Nursery men, outside caterers, hedge cutters, DIY warehouses and miners alike have had their specialist needs met by Slingsby products as have airlines and dockyards. Whilst there still remains an impressive range of products that involve manual handling, many a hospital porter and mailroom staff are grateful for the company's range of powered platform trucks.

Elsewhere loft ladders, tea trolleys and hotel chamber maids' trolleys are Slingsby-made, as are those simple, low oblong platforms with four sturdy wheels made to shift awkward half ton pianos in narrow corridors. The Slingsby castor is a vital adjunct to the job of moving things with the minimum possible output of muscle power. The late Winston Churchill even had a Slingsby lift installed.

But who was HC Slingsby? And how has the firm he founded in Victorian Bradford evolved through the decades?

Over a century ago the trucks and trolleys moving goods and materials around Bradford's factories and yards were invariably made by H C Slingsby.

Harry Crowther Slingsby worked for the family firm of Wholesale Bottlers in Bradford, established in 1883 and it was during his time in the bottling business that he first started looking into labour saving devices.

It was normal in many factories to haul the raw materials to the top floor and allow gravity to move the products downwards as processing flowed from floor to floor. But this failed to address the horizontal movement of goods and materials along the same level of often enormous floor areas. Until Slingsby started manufacturing trucks and trolleys this was done on locally designed and built equipment mounted on two or more small wheels or even on

sled-like runners. Each industry developed its own variations in style which differed in the weight, shape and composition of the goods moved.

Sack trolleys well-known to farmers, brewers and railway porters were found in every work place in the land including grocery shops in the days when flour, sugar and dried fruit was delivered in large sacks for bagging to order for each shopper.

Simple in design, often clumsy and weighty in appearance, these trolleys were so cleverly made that heavy loads could be moved along a paved surface with relative ease.

Another popular model was the two-wheeled Trek Cart, a high-wheeled flat cart with low sides and a shaft ending in a handle so that one or two people could tow it along. Up until the 1960s one could find Boy Scouts hauling their camping gear along country lanes on them, while naval barracks kept stables of them for sailors to ferry their kit in or for moving equipment around shore establishments without burning petrol.

Street traders of all kinds once carried their produce in or on handcarts - from the once common 'Barrow Boys' to more specialist vehicles once used by postmen and bakers.

These were HC Slingsby's inspiration for a huge variety of designs for every trade. The textile mills required trucks to contain loose, bulky fibres which were ferried about in capacious wicker baskets or rawhide tubs mounted on wheels. These useful all rounder vehicles were built light enough to be pushed or pulled by one person operating in confined spaces so that size was a deciding factor as were the often greasy and uneven floors.

Top left: Harry Crowther Slingsby.
Left: An early view inside HC Slingsby.
Below: 'The Slingsby Mixed Six' - the founder and his five sons pulling various models of a popular Lifting Truck, the forerunner of the modern day Pallet Truck, 1920.

Between 1893 and 1907 the company traded from the works in Joseph Street and subsequently Bath Street, Bradford.

A Paris office opened in 1902. In 1907 a factory was built to order in Preston Street, Bradford. Following the First World War, during which Slingsby equipment was in high demand, Harry Slingsby's eldest son, Cecil joined the business as a Salesman. A year later son Victor joined the company's French connection as a van boy so that he would learn to speak the language as a native. He ran the French area until he, his wife Micette and son Jimmie caught the last ship to leave St. Nazaire as the Germans took over the Unoccupied Zone of France in 1940.

Meanwhile, putting his sons through the mill before being allowed to take charge of running it, Harry Slingsby appointed son Guy as a General Office Clerk in 1924: after 24 years service he became Sales Director. Leo Slingsby, too, made his start in the same lowly way but died of TB a few years later. Harry Slingsby continued to travel the world whilst his sons, nephew Geoffrey and his brother, Walter

Top: *The company's early accounts office.* **Right:** *H C Slingsby former premises: The Bath Street works (top left), the works on Listerhills Road (top right), the Preston Street Works circa 1920s (bottom left) and 2002 (bottom right).*

Slingsby managed the day to day business. In the 1920s the 'Slingsby Rolla Rocka Lift Truck' was a patented design developed to load and lift half a ton in only five seconds, as easily as a standard hand truck that would normally handle only 200 lbs. The 'Rolla Rocka' used the force of gravity to form part of the lifting motion, taking a significant amount of effort away from the operator. This truck was a real 'work horse' until the end of the 1960s when it was superseded by the hand hydraulic Pallet Lift Truck still in common use today.

Loft ladders were also introduced in the 1920s as one of the many innovations that Harry Slingsby was developing and patenting to keep his firm ahead of competitors. As soon as Slingsby's protective patent licenses ran out competitors, including former employees who knew a thing or two about truck-making, would copy the Slingsby models and try to undersell them.

Designs have come and gone as working practices and labour saving machines have evolved resulting in new methods and means of moving and lifting materials and goods. Cast iron and heavy timbers have given way to tubular and sheet steel, aluminium and plastic. Meanwhile HC Slingsby has striven to maintain its position as a front-runner in the materials handling industry with enthusiasm, a legacy passed on by HC himself.

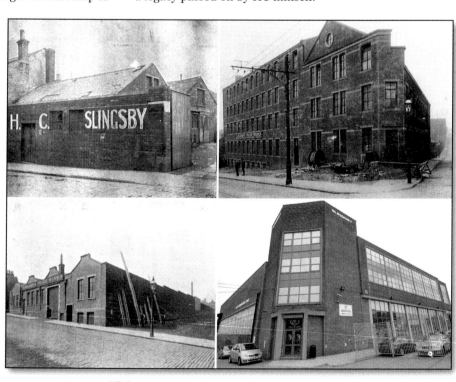

the wider market. The Slingsby catalogue now has 1,345 pages with over 35,000 products on offer.

In 1991 the company added a new dimension to its manufacturing capabilities with the installation of a Rotational moulding plant. Initially to produce Mobile Plastic Containers, the company now also produces Litter Bins, Salt/Grit bins and other material handling products.

The business moved into a new home in Otley Road, Baildon in 2005/6. The company is now installed in state of the art offices with a brand new warehouse facility.

Today the company's profile has changed from being primarily a manufacturer to that of a distribution business, though one which still retains a niche manufacturing capability.

However with such a long experience of supplying solutions to business, H C Slingsby's philosophy of helping his customers maximise their efficiency by saving time and money still remains true for the company in today's rapidly changing marketplace. Just as old 'HC' aimed to do, the company is still able to offer tailor-made product or solutions for its customers, from either its own design and build facility or through its vast resource capability - which now stretches right across the world.

Unsurprisingly the customer base has evolved to include modern Leisure Centres, Sports Complexes and the Service Industries. These have added to the traditional customer base such as the Manufacturing Industry, Health Authorities, Local and Regional Government bodies, the Ministry of Defence and the Hotel and Food Service markets.

Even automated factory production lines need Slingsby trucks and trolleys at the beginning and end of the manufacturing processes.

Slingsby launched the first edition of its Industrial and Commercial products catalogue 'The Slingsby Trading Post' in 1981. The 16-page catalogue offered for sale by mail order various items of industrial and commercial equipment of non-Slingsby origin to provide an industrial products selection service to supplement the supply of traditional Slingsby manufactured goods. The catalogue was issued twice a year and quickly became a successful addition to the sales effort. So much so that subsequent publications included the full Slingsby own manufactured range. In this way Slingsby was able to very quickly introduce products to

The business of keeping industry and commerce moving is still the major goal of HC Slingsby plc today.

Top left: *Storage facility at Preston Works.*
Centre: *Rotational moulding, 2007.*
Below: *HC Slingsby's new premises, Otley Road, Baildon, Shipley.*

Sydney Packett & Sons - Past, Present and Future

Mr. Packett should be advanced whatever sum he required. Business went well and the overdraft was soon paid off.

Yet another early difficulty was the need to go out and seek business during the day. This meant that that the office was left empty. Mrs Packett was helpful, manning the office when she could, but full time assistance was obviously needed. Mr Packett was glad to secure the services of a young clerk, Kenneth Fox. Unfortunately Mr Fox was away from work for four months with pneumonia during his first year. Kenneth Fox returned however, eventually to become a director.

Before long an arrangement was made with J W Ackroyd & Son, jointly to do commercial and private house inventories

When the long-established Bradford insurance brokers Sydney Packet & Sons Ltd moved out of its city centre offices to new premises at Salts Wharf in Shipley it took over 500 packing cases to carry 80 years of business to the firm's new home.

The firm's beginnings were not auspicious. It was in 1920 that Sydney Packett gave £20 for the key to a small room on the third floor of No. 1, Ivegate, Bradford. However, the firm next door, which sold ladies' blouses, had the lock removed and a new one fitted whilst Sydney was out. As a result he had to go to court before he could set up his business as an insurance broker on his 33rd birthday.

There was no chance of a separate telephone in those days. Fortunately, the architect on the floor below, a Mr. Atkinson, kindly agreed to let Sydney share a joint line.

Sydney's most pressing concern however was money. The manager of Martin's Bank in Tyrrel Street asked for security against a possible loan but Sydney had none. However he mentioned that Colonel Morris of Halifax, a director of the bank, would speak for him. The colonel recommended that

and valuations and to undertake fire loss settlements. This was very hard work, but the fees made Mr Packett a modest living and built up the insurance side of the business. Soon he was able to visit his clients in a car with a chauffeur, which was fortunate as he did not hold a driving licence.

With several others, Sydney formed the Insurance Advisory Section of Bradford Chamber of Commerce in 1927. For many years he was a member of the committee and served a term as Chairman.

A move was made to more spacious premises in Lloyds Bank Chambers, Hustlergate, Bradford in 1928, from where the firm would operate for many decades, eventually occupying three floors.

In the 1930s competition for business was very keen. There were more insurance brokers in Bradford compared with the population than any other city in the country.

Sydney Packett had been a member of Bradford Wool Exchange for some time. The Exchange thronged with representatives of the textile and associated industries and insurance men abounded as members. Soon Sydney was appointed to act as broker and adviser to one of the largest textile groups in the country.

In the 1930s Sydney Packett became a city councillor, he served on the Baths Committee and the Conditioning

Top left facing page: Mr Sydney Packett, founder of the company, in a photograph dating from the mid 1930s.
Left facing page: Bradford's Wool Exchange where Sydney Packett was appointed to act as broker and adviser to one of the largest textile groups in the country.
Above: Mr Neville Packett.
Above right: Mr Sydney Duncan Packett.
Right: Mr Neville Packett receiving the Royal Medal of Merit (Silver) from H. M. The King of Tonga.

The Packetts served a year as Deputy Lord Mayor and Lady Mayoress of Bradford (1940-41), although in wartime the purely social engagements were severely restricted. That year their elder son, Charles Neville Packett joined the firm as a junior before volunteering for the army in 1941.

In March 1942 the firm became a private limited company, Sydney Packett & Sons Ltd., with Sydney as Governing Director, the other directors being Charles Neville Packett and Kenneth Fox. The founder's younger son, Sydney Duncan Packett, like his brother, served in the firm for a short period before joining the RAF. Both sons returned to the family business after the war and Duncan too became a director.

The business was able to expand rapidly in the 1950s. In Festival of Britain year (1951) a contract was obtained from the British Wool Marketing Board, followed by the National Pig Progeny Testing Board and the Potato Marketing Board. The firm would eventually have the privilege of accounts

House, Transport and Watch Committees. He did voluntary work in the administration of Public Assistance, as well as being President of the Insurance Institute of Bradford (1930-31) and was a long-serving member of the Yorkshire and North Eastern District Committee of the Corporation of Insurance Brokers. He took an interest in Bradford City Boys' Club, founding and serving on its committee.

On the outbreak of the second world war Sydney Packett formed the Wool Insurance Committee with two other brokers, to advise the industry and deal with Marine Insurance for the Wool Control.

The war brought with it staff shortages, petrol rationing and Excess Profits Tax! It was agreed by the members of the Corporation of Brokers that they would not solicit business from one another so it was not easy for Sydney to expand his business during this period. Constantly changing and inexperienced staff made it difficult even to service the existing clients satisfactorily. Kenneth Fox, and the unrelated Miss Irene Fox who joined Sydney as cashier in 1931 and served faithfully until her marriage in 1964, were pillars of strength.

*Above: Hustlergate, Bradford, home of Sydney Packett & Sons Ltd from 1928 to 2000. **Right:** A brochure dating from 1980s.*

with two hundred authorities and Training and Enterprise Councils.

In the early 1950s the firm decided it needed its own full-time fire surveyor and so, in 1954, a separate Fire Department and also an Accident Department were established.

Neville Packett made the first of his many long-distance 'prospecting' trips in 1962.

That year, the Land and Marine Risk Commodity Insurance business of the Australian Wheat Board was obtained. This huge account was secured after lengthy negotiations and against keen competition. In the following year. Neville visited Australia to service the Wheat Board connection. On the

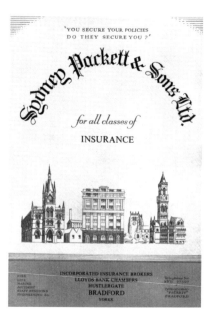

same extensive journey he managed to win business from the Australian Egg Board. To mark his travels to and interest in the Pacific, he received the Order of the Pacific from the Pacific Area Travel Association.

In 1964, the purchase of Frederick C. Wolfe & Son Ltd. meant the opening of a London office. Finally in 1964 when the first of the Industrial Training Boards was set up, the firm was entrusted with the Board's insurance arrangements. Subsequently it acted for most of the other ITBs.

The firm celebrated its Golden Jubilee on 1st March 1970 with a party. Business continued to flourish at home and abroad. In 1973, Mr. Duncan's elder son, Charles, the founder's first grandson, joined the firm, starting, like all the other members of the family, as a junior clerk.

In the New Year's Honours List the following year, 'Mr Neville' was made an MBE.

When, in March 1977, Sydney Packett celebrated his 90th birthday, the staff gave a dinner for him at the Bradford Club. Later in the year, his second grandson, Andrew, joined the firm.

Sydney Packett & Sons Ltd celebrated sixty years of insurance business on 1st March 1980 with the founder now aged 93. He remained active until his death on 11th December 1980.

During the company's long history it has developed a strong reputation for the quality of its insurance advice. As its clients' business activities vary, continued close contact with them helps to develop a full understanding of their particular insurance needs and enables the company to tailor a more efficient professional and comprehensive personal service unique to them.

As a consequence the firm has developed a number of specialist areas and are now the foremost provider of insurance related products to the Training Industry within the UK. Another area of their expertise is in the Charity Sector where the organization is one of the largest brokers in this field and represents some of the best known Charities in the country.

Now in the 21st century Sydney Packett & Sons Ltd bears little resemblance to the firm of the 1950 and 60s. The company is now one of the north's largest truly independent insurance brokers and is able to give specialist advice in all areas of insurance.

The integrity and financial strength of a company is critical to its success. A measure of its integrity is Sydney Packett & Sons' association with, and membership of, the Insurance Brokers' Registration Council, the British Insurance & Investment Brokers' Association, and is authorised and regulated by the Financial Services Authority. The ultimate endorsements however are to be found in the records of thousands of satisfied clients, carried to Shipley in those 500 packing cases.

Top, both pictures: The impressive Sydney Packett & Sons Ltd's Salts Wharf premises, Shipley. **Below:** Directors Charles and Andrew Packett.

Holmes Mann - Packaged to Perfection

Today in the 21st century Holmes, Mann & Co Ltd is one of the best known names in the packaging industry. It was in 1890 that Jonas Holmes and Matthew Mann moved into 202 Leeds Road in Bradford and started the business we know today. Recognising the potential of the site they occupied, they remained in business there for the next 40 years. They were experienced in the packing case trade and soon had orders flowing in from Bradford's then bustling wool industry.

Jonas Holmes, the great grandfather of the company's present Managing Director, was the son of John Jonas Holmes, a local journeyman case maker.

At the time the partnership was formed Jonas was 35 years old. According to the 1891 census he described himself as a sawmill machinist born in Hounsworth, Yorkshire: curiously in the census ten years earlier he had been working as a case maker and claimed to have been born in Toftshaw in Yorkshire. On more certain ground Jonas had previously been the foreman at a nearby firm of casemakers before leaving to join what was at first the partnership of Holmes, Mann, Bennett, Bransfield and Cook based in Bradford's Lower Ernest Street.

By the time the fledgling firm moved to Leeds Road in 1890 the partnership was down to just two: Jonas Holmes and Matthew Mann. Possibly these were the only two partners who had got along with each other. Certainly the fact that they jointly shared a pony and trap suggests that they could work with each other without trouble. Or perhaps it was simply that with Jonas owning 4/7ths of the firm compared to his partner's 3/7ths that there was no room for argument.

Early on they decided to add rolling boards for cloth to their stock-in-trade and so became members of the Bradford Rolling Board and Packing Case Makers Society. This association had very strict rules which had to be read and understood because no-one was allowed to "plead ignorance in case of breach thereof".

Members who lost their copy had to pay 3d for another one, a not inconsiderable sum in

Top left: Jonas Holmes.
Right: Matthew Mann.
Below: An early company letterhead.

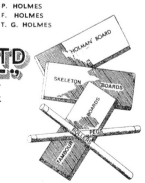

TELEPHONE BRADFORD 25212

BUSINESS ESTABLISHED 1890

Directors :
P. HOLMES
F. HOLMES
T. G. HOLMES

HOLMES, MANN & CO. LTD,

MANUFACTURERS OF ROLLING BOARDS, TIN, ZINC & WOOD CASES.

Speciality 3 PLY RETURNABLE CASES.

HARRIS STREET SAWMILLS
BRADFORD,
YORKS. BD1 5HZ

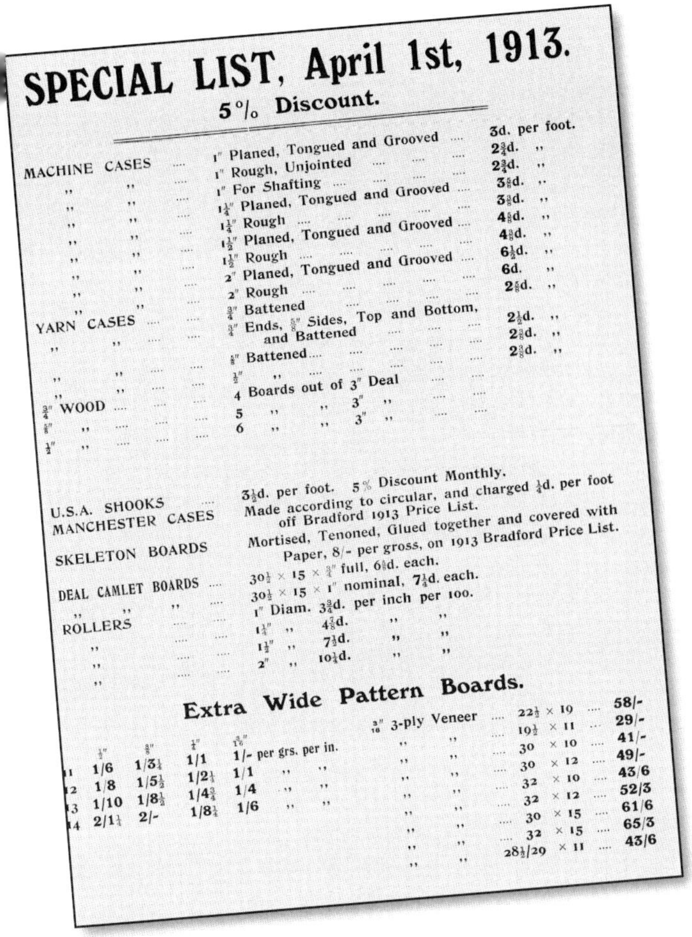

SPECIAL LIST, April 1st, 1913.

5% Discount.

MACHINE CASES	1" Planed, Tongued and Grooved	3d. per foot.
" "	1" Rough, Unjointed	2¾d. "
" "	1" For Shafting	2¾d. "
" "	1¼" Planed, Tongued and Grooved	3⅝d. "
" "	1¼" Rough	3⅜d. "
" "	1½" Planed, Tongued and Grooved	4⅝d. "
" "	1½" Rough	4⅜d. "
" "	2" Planed, Tongued and Grooved	6½d. "
" "	2" Rough	6d. "
" "	¾" Battened	2⅝d. "
YARN CASES	¾" Ends, ⅝" Sides, Top and Bottom, and Battened	2½d. "
" "	⅝" Battened	2⅜d. "
" "	½" "	2⅜d. "
¾" WOOD	4 Boards out of 3" Deal	
⅝" "	5 " " 3" "	
½" "	6 " " 3" "	

U.S.A. SHOOKS	3½d. per foot. 5% Discount Monthly.
MANCHESTER CASES	Made according to circular, and charged ¼d. per foot off Bradford 1913 Price List.
SKELETON BOARDS	Mortised, Tenoned, Glued together and covered with Paper, 8/- per gross, on 1913 Bradford Price List.
DEAL CAMLET BOARDS	30½ × 15 × ¾" full, 6⅝d. each.
" " "	30½ × 15 × 1" nominal, 7¼d. each.
ROLLERS	1" Diam. 3¾d. per inch per 100.
"	1¼" " 4⅞d. " "
"	1½" " 7½d. " "
"	2" " 10¼d. " "

Extra Wide Pattern Boards.

	½"	⅜"	¼"	3/16"
11	1/6	1/3¼	1/1	1/- per grs. per in.
12	1/8	1/5½	1/2¼	1/1 " "
13	1/10	1/8½	1/4¾	1/4 " "
14	2/1¼	2/-	1/8¼	1/6 " "

3/16" 3-ply Veneer	22½ × 19	58/-
" "	19½ × 11	29/-
" "	30 × 10	41/-
" "	30 × 12	49/-
" "	32 × 10	43/6
" "	32 × 12	52/3
" "	30 × 15	61/6
" "	32 × 15	65/3
" "	28½/29 × 11	43/6

those days. The members' dues stood at 7d per week and if arrears exceed 8 shillings the man would be withdrawn from the shop. The member's contributions would also be refused if he did not bring along his card for them to be recorded.

In those days the Society allowed no boy over 16 to be taken on unless he had worked in the trade before. The men worked a standard 50 hour week from 7am until 5.30 pm with half an hour for breakfast and an hour for dinner. In 1905 a new rule was introduced: One boy will be allowed to work at Casemaking to every three men 20 years and over.

During the 1920s Holmes Mann moved from horses and carts to motorised vehicles – a massive step forward in both comfort and efficiency. Amazingly the stabling and hay storage areas used for the horses can still be seen at the factory today. The new vehicles were well received by both drivers and customers, and were shown off at every opportunity, even if, with their manual starters, solid wooden seats, lack of doors, windows, heaters and radios, they seem primitive by today's standards.

Percy Holmes was once approached by one of the wagon drivers complaining bitterly of the cold and the lack of any form of heating in the wagons. Realising there was little he could do Percy tried to appease the driver with the words 'Don't worry lad, it's only winter for half the year'!

In 1930 the business moved to Hammerton Street and during the war years it took orders from the Munitions Supply Company making boxes and grenade holders.

The firm remained a partnership for many years until it was decided to turn the business into a limited company. The words Holmes, Mann & Co Ltd were painted on the chimney in anticipation of the event – sadly Jonas Holmes died the day before the incorporation was due to take place.

It would be Jonas' son Percy Holmes who would take the firm forward, together with his son Gordon.

In 1950 Percy and Gordon Holmes paid £4,000 to the Mann family for the use of their name in the new company Holmes, Mann and Co Ltd. That same year the company

Above left: *A Holmes Mann price list dating from 1913.* ***Below:*** *A 1970 delivery truck outside the company's Duncombe Way warehouse.*

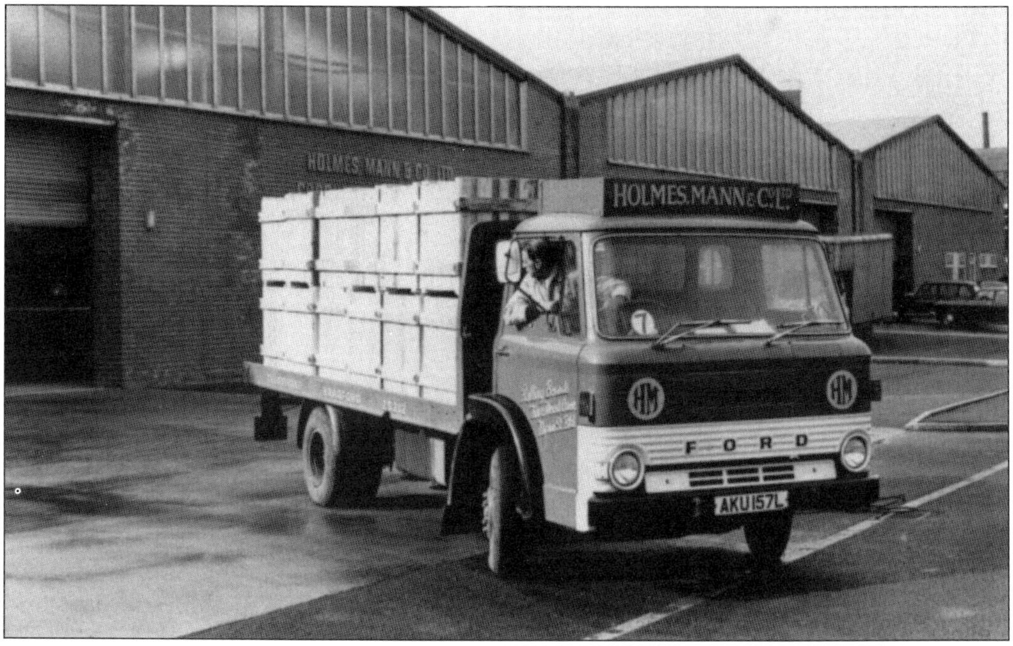

opened its present site in Harris Street. The company's origin in a partnership of five is commemorated in the comma which still forms an integral part of the company's correct title.

Such was demand for packaging that at one point the firm had as many as 120 employees. Today with modern machinery and technology this has fallen to a leaner 42.

The old handsaws have long since been replaced by computer-controlled crosscut saws and the latest packaging machinery such as case tapers and stretch wrappers are now supplied.

Today the firm is a supplier to many industries, including light engineering, food and the fabrics and plastics industries. It produces a large range of packaging products so that customers can be offered a 'one stop shop' solution to most of their packaging requirements.

The firm specialises in bespoke pallets, cases and combination packs. Several local companies produce some items that overlap with those of Holmes Mann, but none of them produce the whole range.

The company has been set some interesting challenges over the years. In 1989 wooden packing cases with polystyrene fittings were made to transport portraits of HRH Prince Charles from Dean Clough in Halifax to London. Some years ago Holmes Mann manufactured a huge, and virtually flat, packing case for a metal gasket which was used by Red Adair to extinguish a North Sea oilrig fire.

The largest packing case or crate within living memory was made to pack gas separators for Abu Dhabi. The crates were as large as many houses, 40 feet long, 14 feet high, and had to be assembled on site around the gas separators before being given a police escort to the docks.

Other more unusual commissions have included a 7 metre long stepped pallet for shipping machinery abroad, and also a large packing case, with polyethylene foam lined drawers, hinges and returnable irons.

Customer service and product quality of its transit packaging products are still pursued above all else

Holmes Mann remains an expert manufacturer of bespoke wooden packing cases, crates and pallets, designed to customers' exact specifications.

Certification by the UK Wood Packaging Material Marking Programme (UKWPMMP) means that its heat-treated timber stock meets strict ISPM15 plant health requirements so its timber products are suitable for export to China, North America, Australia, New Zealand and many other destinations.

Above: *A Holmes Mann service engineer's van from the 1990s.* ***Left:*** *One of the company's stretch wrapping machines.*

In addition to its standard and bespoke timber pallets and cases, the company also provides related products such as frames, shelf decking, cradles and platforms.

Holmes Mann can produce a broad range of corrugated cases, from small die cut boxes all the way up to heavy duty triple-wall cartons with bespoke pallets, in a variety of different board grades and finishes.

The firm also manufactures spiral tubes and straight wound (convolute) tubes in-house at its Bradford factory. Holmes Mann also has its own printing facilities, enabling it to provide three-colour printed spiral wound tubes as well as in-house tape printing facility for printing self-adhesive packaging tapes.

Using the latest core-cutting technology very short tubes suitable for ribbons and tapes and many other applications can be produced.

An extensive range of packaging materials is kept in stock, including a wide selection of self-adhesive tapes, cushioning products, such as bubble wrap and foam, stretch film, polypropylene strap, loose fill, and many other end of line packaging materials.

Holmes Mann are also pleased to be UK distributors for the Siat range of packaging machinery, which includes carton sealers, stretch-wrappers and carton erectors. The firm also supplies associated products such as conveyors and ink jet coders, and consumable products for use with the machines. There is a showroom in Bradford with a wide range of machines on display.

The company carries an extensive range of Siat spare parts and has its own engineers for service and call out to machinery.

Today with Paul and Simon representing the current generation of the Holmes family the company looks forward to the future with a confidence born of more than century in business.

Left: *Paul Holmes.*
Below: *A complete packaging line in the Holmes Mann showroom.*

The Girls' Grammar School, Bradford
Education for the 21st Century

As early as the 17th century it was declared that there should be 'one free Grammar School of King Charles at Bradford for the teaching, instructing, and better bringing up of children and youth in Grammar and other good Learning and Literature'. But despite that noble statement there were no secondary schools for girls in the city of Bradford even by the mid 19th century.

The passing of the 1869 Endowed Schools Act opened the way to establish just such a school, and it was down to the efforts of a dedicated group of citizens including WE Forster, the MP for Bradford, Mrs Byles and the Ladies' Educational Association, that £5,000 was raised.

On 29th September 1875 The Girls' Grammar School, Bradford was formally opened by Lady Frederick Cavendish in the already cramped Hallfield Road School, a soot-blackened, converted building, attached to Busby's.

The first students were mainly the daughters of professional men and the merchant families of the Manningham area who paid the sum of 4 guineas a term, twelve guineas per annum; no extras... Through the generosity of Sir Titus Salt and Mr Henry Brown scholarships were made available for girls from less well off families to aspire to the newly-opening colleges in Oxford, Cambridge and London.

The first headmistress, Miss Porter, wanted pupils to be able to think for themselves and not be crammed with a mere smattering of knowledge, although she did not go as far as the local newspaper which envisaged the school training up girls fit to be intelligent companions for intelligent men. The school was one of the first in the country to include Physical Education in its curriculum.

In 1887 the Examiner for the Oxford and Cambridge Schools' Examination Board wrote:

My experience of Girls' Schools is not wide, but Bradford's easily bears the palm and if I compare it with the Boys' School in the subjects done in common-Elementary Mathematics, Geography, History and English Literature – Bradford girls more than hold their own... The intelligence and sharpness of the girls seemed to me to be decidedly above the average.

The School Chronicles of those years provide not only a rich record of life at BGGS but also a history of girls' education in the late 19th and early 20th century.

These extracts are from the 1890s:

In those days we began each morning with four order marks and lost one every time we broke a rule. Of course if we lost four during the first lesson we felt we could behave as we liked for the remainder of the day.

Then there were terrible Tuesday afternoons with Lower V.A English Grammar followed by Macaulay's essay on the younger Pitt... Janet Allen waving a defiant plait and May Wheat fixing me with an uncompromising eye saying 'That is not how Miss Clement did it'

Top left: *Miss Mary E Porter, Headmistress 1875 - 1880*
Left: *An early view of the Girls' Grammar School, Bradford.*
Above: *A staff photograph from June 1894, Miss Stocker, Headmistress centre, Miss Sharp front row right.*

A girl should never be allowed to dawdle about the first part of an evening and then make lessons an excuse for stopping up late. Girls should not be allowed to visit so much during term time.

I remember the first Board of Education Inspection when a pupil asked the characteristically pertinent question 'Are they coming for us or for you Miss Savill?'

Many girls who attended this school kept very late hours... all the best work that was done in the school, almost without a single exception, was done by those girls who went to bed in good time.

In the Jubilee Celebrations of 1925 the school had much to be proud of, and many tributes to pay to the women, Headmistresses, staff, Governors and Old Girls who had in the face of much prejudice shown what girls' education could achieve. In particular the debt was acknowledged for the inspirational leadership of its three headmistresses, Miss Porter, second to none as both teacher and organiser, Miss Stocker, awe inspiring and original in thought, and Miss Roberts, who was Headmistress from 1894 to 1927 and who inspired deep love and reverence amongst staff and pupils alike.

Tribute was also paid to two of the original Board of Governors, Lady Byles and Mr Titus Salt, and to Mr Duncan Law the first chair of Governors, whose daughter Margaret

Law was present during the celebrations and who worked tirelessly for the school.

For the pupils themselves a new world was opening up. Letters from Old Girls studying at the women's colleges of Oxford, Cambridge and London provide a fascinating insight into the career opportunities opening up for women in the first part of the 20th century.

BGGS girls were also venturing out into the world, travelling widely in America, Africa, Europe and Asia. They went as teachers, sometimes as missionaries, and they were always prepared to write back to the school inspiring others.

But despite these pioneers, in 1916 Miss Roberts was to make a special plea to parents to encourage their daughters to look beyond the home as a career.

The School Honours Board pays tribute to the generations of girls who pioneered careers for women before the first world war becoming doctors, lawyers, headmistresses of other girls' schools and university lecturers.

The first world war was a turning point for women. Many Old Girls served as doctors and nurses at home and on the front lines in France, Egypt and Palestine. School life continued as normally as possible with the addition of knitting socks for servicemen, making sandbags, collecting moss for wound-dressings and sending parcels to prisoners of war. The school also took in and supported Belgian refugees.

Meanwhile the buildings did not match the school's growing success.

In 1927 an appeal was launched by the new Headmistress, Miss Hooke, to raise money and in 1929 the Preparatory Department moved into the newly-purchased estate of Lady Royd whilst plans were drawn up for a purpose-built school in its 17 acres. It was 1936 before the new buildings could be opened by the Princess Royal. Instead of the 'dark and gloomy classrooms' of the old building, pupils now had airy and spacious rooms and corridors, a library with Thompson 'mouse furniture' tables and chairs, a gymnasium, a hall, art rooms and laboratories.

Prominent in those early years was one girl who fought in the school mock election of 1929 as a Labour candidate, winning just 29 votes! The rebellious Barbara Betts became Head Girl and went to St Hugh's College, Oxford and then

In her introduction to the Centenary Chronicle Miss Black wrote:

The first century of the school has coincided with the movement to establish first the rights of women to be educated as men, and then their right to equal opportunities to use their education in work. Women from this school have always been at the forefront of this struggle. We have no need to apologise for the values and educational standards we maintain. Sometimes we must lean against the wind.

In the years following the Centenary the school under the leadership of Miss Gleave (1975-86) and the present headmistress Mrs LJ Warrington, has continued to maintain the principles of its founders and to build upon the high educational standards achieved, providing breadth and excellence in its academic curriculum, and offering a wealth of extra-curricular activities in sport, drama, art, music and engineering.

The school has remained convinced of the benefits of single-sex education for girls and the high position it has maintained in the school league tables have more than justified that belief. It still remains true to the ethos expounded by Miss Black in 1975:

What emerges is that the changes in the outward fashions of living do not conceal the continuity of the spirit of the school, its independence, social concern, intellectual vigour, and capacity to adapt.

on to become the prominent Labour politician Barbara Castle. She paid a memorable visit to the school in the late 1990s and was still able to inspire sixth form students with her fiery enthusiasm. In her memory the Old Girls donated a statuette, aptly called the Red Queen, awarded annually to the girl who displays the greatest independence of spirit and mind.

In the Second World War part of the school was evacuated to Settle until 1940. Pupils and staff were actively involved in charity work, whilst many Old Girls served in the armed forces. The junior school became a rest centre for evacuated women and children from the south.

In the decades leading up to the centenary celebrations in 1975 the school went from strength to strength under the leadership of Miss Hooke (1927-55) and Miss Black 1955-75).

Above left: Lady Royd, The Preparatory School, photographed from the Millennium Garden. Left: The sixth form of 1926. Barbara Betts - the late Baroness Castle - seated right end. Top: The new School opened in 1936 by the Princess Royal. Above: Lessons can be fun. Right: Girls enjoy the sunshine in the quad.

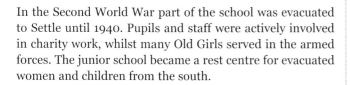

G W Butler - Muck & Brass

'Where there's muck there's brass' is one of those proud Yorkshire sayings which harks back to the days when Bradford's skyline was dominated by smoking chimney stacks. Most of the mills may be gone, but there's still brass to be made in scrap and waste disposal. Today the most prominent name in the field is that of GW Butler Ltd.

GW Butler Ltd has changed dramatically down the years, with great success in the 1940s and 1950s, and a major boom in the 1960s. A decline started in the mid-1970s, but due to diversifying into general waste in the 1990s, and clinical waste disposal in the late-1990s GW Butler Ltd is today a highly successful waste management company.

Throughout its history the company has been run by Butler family members. It has had had differing levels of staff down the years however: more than forty were employed during the scrap metal boom in the 1960s.

There have been three sites in GW Butler Ltd's company history – Ellar Ghyll in Menston from the late 1920s until early 1970s – Bowling Ironworks Bradford from 1933 until 2004 – and Bow Beck Bradford from 2003 until the present day.

Company founder, George William Butler, born in 1882, was son of James William Butler from Pontefract. James William, a painter and decorator, moved to Menston when he got the job of decorating High Royds Hospital.

A typical Victorian stickler, George William Butler was very thrifty and held firm Victorian values: no talking during Sunday lunch and all family members required to be present, including the housekeeper who was called 'Aunty Alice. He was very strict with his family: when one son got married he gave the happy couple £50; his son said 'thank you' and said he would be back after a week spent on honeymoon, to which George's response was that if he wasn't back at work on Monday he would be out of a job! He was a typical Yorkshire businessman and very careful with money: he even haggled for a cash discount when he wanted to buy items at a well-known London store.

George William Butler started trading using a horse and cart in and around Menston collecting scrap which led to the purchase of Ellar Ghyll (Menston) in the 1920s. It

remained in the family until the early 1970s when it was purchased by the local council, though it remains a waste disposal site.

In 1933 GW Butler purchased a large part of Bowling Ironworks, and the main part of the company was run from this site until it was sold in 2004. During the 1940s until the 1960s GW Butler Ltd was one of the largest scrap metal merchant in Yorkshire.

GW Butler had five sons and always stressed that 'always pick up small bits of scrap lad and the big bits will look after themselves'. Four sons worked for the company – Jack, George (Tommy), Henry (Harry) and Wilfred. Jack's children John and Jill joined the company for a short period. George's (Tommy) sons Jerry and Jimmy and daughter Judith also joined along with Henry's (Harry) son Andrew.

During the war the company was as considered an essential service for the war effort, as a consequence GW Butler's sons were not conscripted but Wilfred and Jimmy (the fifth son, who did not join the company) joined the army. Tommy and Harry were both members of the Voluntary reserves.

It was suggested by Tommy Butler that when business was successful in the 1940s that George William should purchase a Rolls Royce, his response was 'It'll nobbut get me from A to B same as any other car, so why have an expensive car.'

Top left: *Founder, George William Butler.* **Left:***Mr & Mrs GW Butler (top) and family pictured in the 1930s.* **Below:** *The company's old Bowling Ironworks site in the 1940s.*

Harry ran the Bowling Ironworks Yard. Jack ran the Ellar Ghyll site in Menston, but also went out and purchased scrap. Wilf Butler worked at the Iron Mongers shop (Hicks Fearns), that side of the business was sold off to pay GW Butler's death duties in 1955. Wilf then became company secretary at GW Butler Ltd.

In the 1950s during the Suez Crisis when fuel was rationed George (Tommy) did not want this to affect getting to work so he rode his horse, Ben, to work from Menston: it was reported in the Telegraph & Argus. Tommy was well known around Bradford as he was chairman of Bradford Park Avenue, a good team in those days, but he was also known for his love of big American cars and could often be seen driving round Bradford in his beloved Cadillac Eldorado.

After the war Jack Butler then went round all the war departments quoting for removal of all the defunct war machinery.

In those post-war years when the decline in the wool trade began the company sent out gangs of workers to dismantle the machines in the mills. Tommy was in charge of the 'Heavy gangs' - travelling around collecting mills' scrap machines.

At the same time there was a boom in heavy engineering which led to a need for the disposal of various types of scrap metal (turnings, cutting etc). GW Butler's had many contracts at this time with English Electric, International Harvesters, and Croft Engineering. These were annual contracts by tender, where the scrap was taken away by Butlers: the firm paid around £5 per ton for such scrap. It was taken to either Bradford or Menston depot where it was processed by pressing, bailing or crushing. Larger items were cut into 2ft pieces by Oxy-propane cutters, 2 ft being the best size for putting it into the furnaces. The

waste was moved by railway trucks at Bowling Ironworks down to the British Rail sidings at Hammerton Street then onwards to Sheffield. This continued until the mid - 1970s until a wagon hit the railway bridge on Square Street and British Rail decided not to repair the bridge so everything was moved by road.

In the mid-1950s GW Butler Ltd received a lot of old buses from the bus company Samuel Ledgards, this was a well

*Top: The five brother enjoying a drink together in the early 1960s. **Above:** Andrew Butler's three children, Paul, Deanna and Rosalyn playing on the old U boat engine in the mid 1970s. **Left:** GW Butler's Bowling Iron Works, 1990.*

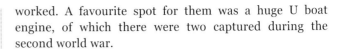

known public transport company which was later taken over by West Yorkshire Bus Co. The old buses were often used for the base of a bonfire at Ellar Ghyll on 5th November: the bonfires were huge, and many Otley and Menston residents would attend the superb 'plot nights'.

In the mid-1960s Jimmy Butler son of George (Tommy) was the first to use a tractor to load scrap metal waste onto wagons - previously this was done with lots of staff using shovels. The first site a tractor was used at was at International Harvester at Five Lane Ends. A second-hand Fordson tractor had been bought and taken up to Harvester but was refused entry as the Fordson was the main competitor of Harvesters. A second-hand Harvester was then purchased in Ripon and driven by Jimmy Butler at 15mph to Five Lane Ends to assist in loading.

In 1972 when Bradford stopped using its trolley-buses GW Butler Ltd got the job of clearing the substations of scrap metal and mercury. This involved taking away all scrap cable etc and dismantling the mercury converters, carefully collecting all mercury into jars as this was a very saleable item.

As children in the mid-1970s the fourth generation of Butlers, Deanna, Paul and Roz spent most Saturdays playing in the scrapyard whilst their father Andrew

worked. A favourite spot for them was a huge U boat engine, of which there were two captured during the second world war.

Fluctuations in scrap prices imposed by British Steel caused problems with the annual contracts especially when there was a drop. The decline of British Engineering in the 1970s caused shutdowns which led on to shortages of scrap. This meant that GW Butler had vehicles that were not being used to their full potential, so the company diversified into general waste collections. By the end of the 1980s and the start of the 1990s general waste became a major part of the business. Wood waste from Newplan on Bowling Back Lane played a large part in this so it was decided to install an incinerator to dispose of such waste. By the mid-1990s this aspect of the business had developed and was now including

the disposal of clinical waste from local hospitals and nursing homes.

Andrew and Jimmy Butler operated the company until their retirements in 2000/2003 when Andrew's daughter Deanna, son Paul and son in law Martin Helstrip took over as directors. The fourth generation of Butlers now runs the company.

*Top: Jimmy Butler, the first to use a tractor to load scrap metal on to wagons. **Below left:** Installation of a GW Butler chimney stack. **Above:** Andrew Butler who moved the company into clinical waste duing the 1990s. **Below:** Interior and exterior views of GW Butler's modern plant in Bowling Back Lane, 2007.*

Kirkgate Shopping Centre - The Centre of Shopping

Folk have been doing their shopping in Bradford for more than eight centuries. The earliest records go back to the 12th century, though no doubt there was buying and selling going on in even earlier times despite William the Conqueror laying waste to the whole area in 1070.

By the reign of Queen Victoria Bradford's heart was its bustling commercial centre filled daily with hordes of shoppers. Since those days the ebb and flow of development has changed the cityscape, but though many buildings may have altered shops and shoppers remain a constant.

With 65 shops and a market - all under cover - there's no better place to shop in Bradford than the Kirkgate Shopping Centre. A multi-million pound refurbishment for the 21st century has created lighter and brighter malls and a striking central dome, specially lit by over 1,400 fibre-optic lights. At the heart of the Dome is BB's Coffee & Muffins, the ideal place to take a break during a visit. It's also where visitors

will find a striking new glass elevator that makes moving from one level to another easier than ever before.

With 550 spaces the Centre's car park, the second largest in the City, is the safest in Bradford and winner of the prestigious AA Secure Car Park Award. Alternatively The Centre is only a few minutes walk from Bradford Interchange rail & bus stations. There is dedicated parking for disabled users and parents with young children and easy access for the disabled people with wheelchair loan available from the Information Bureau.

The Centre was built in 1976 and was one of the original Arndale Centres. Since then it has been refurbished twice - in 1988 and most recently in 2001.

The beginnings of Kirkgate Market go back to 1251 when King Henry III granted to Edmund de Lacy 'that he and his heirs for ever shall have one market every week at his manor of Bradford'.

At first the weekly market, held every Thursday, was run under the auspices of the church, with the old Market Cross in the 'Westgate Box' as a long standing reminder of that fact. Benjamin Rawson who acquired the market rights in the 18th century moved it from Westgate to Market House, Bank Street, bringing to an end the influence of the church – or almost - Sunday opening, now the norm, would still have to wait another couple of hundred years – an interesting reappearance of the Sunday markets held in Bradford in the 14th century.

By 1824 however, the Bank Street site was proving too small and there was a further move to Manor Hall in Kirkgate where the modern story really starts.

At the turn of the 19th Century, Bradford had still been a small rural market town of just 16,000 people, where wool spinning and cloth weaving was carried out in local cottages and farms.

Yet a boom in the textile industry was on the way. By the 1840s there were 38 worsted mills in Bradford town and 70 in the borough. Some two-thirds of the country's wool production was processed in Bradford. By the 1850s Bradford had become the wool capital of the world with a population of 100,000 and with a demand for shops commensurate with its teeming population.

The market at Kirkgate was almost guaranteed to be a success. Yet when stalls were first set up around the once-fine Manor Hall there were a number of objections – reference being made at the time to 'a beggarly array of stalls and shambles'. Shambles is an old word for butchers and slaughterhouses.

The objectors met with little success, and the Kirkgate Market, originally called the Butter Market, has remained on the same site ever since.

By 1976 both phases of the then new Kirkgate Arndale Centre were complete and its backers had persuaded the public that it would be a valuable addition to the city's commercial life. Shopping malls were added to make a complete shopping centre which then remained almost unaltered for the next 14 years.

In 1988 however, refurbishment was deemed necessary: the subsequent work continued for almost a year during which

Left: Kirkgate Market circa 1950s.

the centre still managed to remain open every single day. Once the changes which had cost over three and a half million pounds were complete the site was renamed the Kirkgate Shopping Centre, bounded by Kirkgate, Westgate, Darley Street and Godwin Street.

The car park and the Kirkgate Market were part of the building but belonged to the Bradford Council. The remainder of the centre was owned by the Prudential Insurance Company Ltd. Early in 1987 Prudential Property Management had offered to undertake the refurbishment and produced new plans for the centre.

The centre's tenants were consulted at every stage and their views taken into account. Each week a newsletter was sent to all units to keep occupiers abreast of work in progress. Four Kirkgate Reviews were published to keep the public informed.

New retail units, dubbed Gazebos, were introduced to bring in smaller individual retailers, as well as a Kiddie Ride carousel. An Information Bureau was added, staffed with the management's personnel; the female staff were issued with smart new uniforms of blazers and slacks in keeping with the new image.

Right and below: Interior views of the Kirkgate Shopping Centre in the 1990s (right) and 2007 (below).

By 1997 the Centre had its two main entrances brought up to date and a new logo introduced.

The centre was refurbished in 2001. A new feature dome was installed with its fibre optic lights. The malls now have a bright modern airy feel with clean lines and enhanced lighting. The new scenic lift was installed giving easy access between the two levels of the centre.

The car park was acquired from the council in 2000 and subsequently £1.5 million was spent on improvements providing parent and child spaces as well as more disabled parking spaces. Again the car park is lighter and brighter. It

appliances including printers and monitors as well as water-saving devices in all the toilets throughout the centre.

In addition all cardboard, steel/aluminium and glass are recycled. A scheme is being worked out to recycle coat hangers. All the organic waste from the juice bar goes to Yorkshire Water treatment works at Esholt where it is composted.

A current project is with nine local schools producing teaching resources in the form of Big Books and educational films. The subjects are all social responsibility and crime prevention with the aim of diverting young people from crime.

has won the Park Mark Secure Parking award for five consecutive years and is the safest city centre car park in Bradford.

The centre is host to the Bradford Junior Chamber Christmas Tree appeal which annually collects over 3,000 gifts for needy children in Bradford.

Annual events, such as the model search and the reindeer parade, are family favourites and have become a tradition. The reindeer parade heralds Santa's arrival at his grotto in the centre pulled on his sleigh by real live reindeer. Two young competition winners get to ride in the sleigh with him.

The model search is a competition held each year. Winners in each category get the chance to be put on a modelling agency's books. Several winners have gone on to feature in advertising campaigns. The event is very popular with families and all the children love the chance to 'strut their stuff' on the catwalk.

A refurbishment of the toilets was underway in 2007. A father and baby room was planned to complement the existing mother and baby facilities.

Staff in the centre get involved in various community projects including St Mary's community gardens where cash was provided to attract additional funding from other sources. An eyesore of waste land was then transformed into a well used and safe community garden.

The centre is working to reduce its carbon footprint with assistance from Envirowise. Energy-saving measures include reprogramming lights, switching off all unused

The centre has over 13 million visitors a year with most people visiting at least once a week. Meanwhile retailers change as shopping trends change. The Centre has most recently welcomed Primark which has been an instant hit with Bradford shoppers.

After being in the same ownership since 1987 the centre was sold twice in 2006 and is now in the ownership of Kirkgate Bradford Unit Trust.

The history of shopping in Bradford goes back more than 800 years. Today the city's Kirkgate Shopping Centre is certainly doing its best to add lustre to that long story.

Top: Kirkgate's Big Book project. **Below:** *Two young competition winners get to ride with Santa in his sleigh.*

Uriah Woodhead & Son - Selling Sand to the Arabs

Bradford's premier builders' merchant Uriah Woodhead & Son Ltd has a long and fascinating history. Founded in 1866 by Uriah Woodhead the company has experienced remarkable growth whilst witnessing the extraordinary social and economic change in Bradford over the last century and a half.

Located today on Canal Road and Valley Road the family–run business has an accumulated knowledge of building materials gained from over 140 years of experience. Yet although the business may be long-established its people remain young at heart, maintaining a lively interest in all building activities, and taking a personal interest in all the firm's customers, past, present and potential.

Growth in the last 50 years has gained Uriah Woodhead & Son Ltd a position as one of the largest independent suppliers to the building trade in the north of England.

The business began in Bankfoot, moving to Canal Road (somewhere near the 'P' loop of today) then to warehousers Stewart, Esplen and Greenhough adjacent to Leather Chemical Co Ltd.

The mid 19th century was undoubtedly a good time to start a business dealing in building materials. At the turn of the 19th Century, Bradford was still a small rural market town.

Forty years later however, there were 38 worsted mills in Bradford town and 70 in the borough and two-thirds of the country's wool production was processed in Bradford. By the 1850s Bradford had become the wool capital of the world with a population of 100,000 leading to the development of a solid engineering and manufacturing base, and becoming an important financial centre.

Runaway success led to the rapid expansion of the city. Between 1800 and 1850 Bradford changed from a rural town amongst the woods and fields to a sprawling town filling the valley sides. The town centre expanded and its old buildings were largely replaced by new ones, with lavish Victorian architecture still much in evidence today.

And fully benefiting from that Victorian building boom were builders and builders merchants such as Uriah Woodhead.

Right: *Roofing Sales in the 1960s.*

Uriah Woodhead and his son Irvine owned two large barges called Lion and Tiger which they used to transport cement and other building materials along the Leeds and Liverpool canal and the Bradford Cut. During the late 19th century building sand was taken from George Briggs and Sons quarries at Horsforth and Newlay using horse-drawn block carts and delivered to customers' sites. Subsequently steam engines were used; materials were hauled by railway locomotive and later in the 19th century by the firm's own motor lorries.

In the 1930s the goods yard at Valley Road became the new home to the business.

Irvine Woodhead eventually sold the company to Charles Henry Robinson – affectionately known to all as 'Charlie'. Today Charlie's great great granddaughter, also named Charlie, and her sisters happily play with old model replicas of aggregate suppliers' tipper wagons in the piles of building sand at the firm. Their grandfather John Charles Walker now runs the company: how proud Charlie Robinson would be if he could spy the fifth generation of his family busy playing in the sand.

When John Walker heard the saying 'clogs to clogs in three generations' from his father he quickly shot out and bought himself a pair, much to the annoyance of his father. Now both the fourth and fifth generation have been seen sporting clogs.

During the 1950s Kathleen Walker, John's mother, was a well-known character in Bradford's predominantly male building industry. She ran the business for many years expanding orders by fearlessly climbing building-site ladders to have face-to-face meetings with her customers high up on the scaffolding. In that era she must have caused quite a stir. Today ladies still have an important role in the firm's management, not least in the shape of Pauline Lomax, its General Manager.

In the 1950s and 60s Bradford again began to be transformed, in the same way that it had been in Victorian times. Once again a building boom was underway

Top: A company advert from the early 20th century. Note the lime, laths and hair for plastering, also the limestone and rockery stone by barge from Skipton. *Above right:* Advertising the opening of a new department of Plumbers Merchants in 1977.

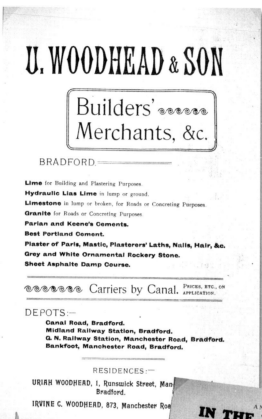

and, exactly as it had 100 years earlier, Uriah Woodhead & Son was at the forefront of supplying materials to those who were doing the work on site.

In the mid-1960s the company was the first in Bradford to acquire a loading shovel and fork lift truck, solely for the speedy and efficient turn around for both customers and suppliers. In those days, long before the current manual weight-handling regulations, such mechanisation was a very welcome addition to the company's equipment. Similarly huge bulk-handling improvements were gained with the development of a fully automated bagging plant in the 1980s.

The creation of the Hardware, Tools and Ironmongery sales counter in the 1970s was an important development for the firm. Shortly afterwards the specialist Plumbing and Heating Sales was opened upstairs at the Canal Road depot. The new Plumbing Manager delighted everyone during the summer by growing tomatoes in display toilet pans. During this period of rapid expansion Uriah Woodhead & Son Ltd began exporting extensively to the Middle East, and was tickled to actually sell sand to the Arabs.

Two excellent customers were Nelson's Builders Merchants in Keighley and its sister company Thomas Nelson and Son (Roofing) Ltd of Bradford – a company like Woodhead's also founded in 1866.

In order to meet demands for timber a sawmill was opened in Valley Road in the 1980s. The 'Street of Building Materials' was opened with a phone box, street signs and a bridge over Bradford Beck to the newly acquired Roofing Material depot of Thomas Nelson & Sons (Roofing) Ltd.

Since then the bridge has witnessed a great deal of traffic over the years. Bradford's builders, joiners, plumbers, roofers, plasterers, drain layers, tilers, DIYers and home improvers continuously pass over the water on their daily

Law Courts, John's Street market to name but a few are amongst the many local buildings to have benefited from materials supplied by the firm. Both figuratively and literally the city of Bradford has grown hand in hand with its most important building materials supplier.

Company policy is to offer comprehensive and satisfactory service to all in the building industry. In particular it aims to service the requirements of builders, plasterers, paviours, drain layers, plumbers, heating specialists, ceramic tilers, roofers – both flat and pitched – joiners, fencers and home improvers. Staff and management are proud to be able to offer large, comprehensive stocks coupled with keen prices, quick delivery and a friendly service.

trek through the yards. The firm's famous Pie, Pea and Pint parties have been thrown on the bridge to celebrate 120th, 121st and 125th anniversaries – as well as Bessie the Loading Shovel's Sad Retirement and Leaving Party. Hundreds of Bradford tradesmen enjoyed the merriment with Pennine Radio's outside broadcasts and horse cart rides a round the city.

In the future of Uriah Woodhead & Son Ltd will no doubt continue to benefit from the virtues of its past still evident in the present: old-fashioned courtesy, knowledge and value. Rightly this independent go-ahead family-run builders' merchant is fiercely proud of its background as one on Bradford's longest established businesses.

Major celebrations have also been marked with the ceremonial firing of the firm's replica Napoleonic cannon. The start of Bradford's half marathon for many years, and Bradford's first festival at the Town Hall, have enjoyed is loud boom.

In 1998 Farrar's Stone Merchant sold Nelsons of Keighley to Uriah Woodhead & Son bringing the benefits of the latter's experience to the building trade in Keighley. Two Jowett Bradford vans in the full livery of the two established Bradford and Keighley merchants can frequently be seen on the roads in the Aire Valley.

Top: Hundreds of Bradford tradesmen enjoyed horse cart rides a round the city at Bessie the Loading Shovel's Sad Retirement and Leaving Party. **Below:** An aerial view of Uriah Woodhead & Son Ltd's Valley Road premises.

Though it may have had a small start back in the reign of Queen Victoria today Uriah Woodhead & Son is a very large undertaking. Today the Canal Road/Valley Road depot covers about five acres with some 70,000 square feet of warehousing all devoted to builders' merchandise.

Some idea of the scale of the business can be gained from checking its stock. At the last attempted count of the stock the team got to 16,000 items and then lost count: hardly surprising when there is over a million pounds of stock held there at any one time. Nor is it surprising to discover that the builders working on prestigious and beautiful buildings of Bradford's historic past were supplied by Uriah Woodhead & Son Ltd: Listers Mill, the Wool Exchange, the Cathedral, Bradford Royal Infirmary, Cartwright Hall, the

Bombay Stores - Celebrating 40 Years
A World of Experience

Everyone enjoys a rags to riches story This is that of a 21-year-old lad who came to Bradford to make his fortune and succeeded. Today Bradford's famous Bombay Stores is serving its third generation of Bradford clients – the children and grandchildren of its first customers. But customers are not restricted only to Bradford: from the heart of the city this once small business is now reaching out to world markets.

In post-war Britain with its booming industries there was a desperate need for semi-skilled staff to fill the jobs that many rejected. In answer to this call came Abdul Kader. He arrived in Bradford in 1957 with just £50 to keep him going while he sought work.

The Northern cities then had a polyglot racial mixture of Jews and Poles who had fled the Nazis, plus post war refugees from Eastern Europe and the once independent Ukraine fleeing the Communists. This heady cultural mix was capped in the late forties and early fifties by Italians who also sought temporary work in the throbbing textile mills.

Christian West Indians, who had enjoyed the benefits of English-style school and examination systems, were also already well established in various cities as public transport workers and hospital auxiliaries by the time Abdul Kader arrived. They, and the Pakistani and Indian immigrants like Abdul Kader, came to live in towns with a climate, not to

mention a dialect, which even southerners from places like London considered extreme. The food was not a bit like mother's back home; the only Mosque in all Britain at the time was in London! The language difficulty was as real a poser as any other migrant finds in a new country where they stand out like a sore thumb, think on t'problem of being a Pom in Oz in the 1950s.

It was tough; but the young Abdul Kader did what go-getters faced with problems do best: he worked hard, first of all as a bus conductor with responsibility for ticket sales and accounting, driver liaison and passenger safety on the open-platform buses of the time. Within six years he had saved sufficient money to pay the deposit on a former fish and chip shop, on offer for a thousand pounds. He continued to work double shifts on the buses whilst his wife, Maryam Kader, put in similar hours as a dressmaker in their corner drapery shop at 306 Great Horton Road.

The early immigrant's thirst for fabrics and Asian wear was the opportunity that Mr and Mrs Kader took advantage of when they started the corner shop operation in 1967.

Initially sourcing of products for the business was done through wholesalers in the Manchester area;

*Left: Family and staff pose with the Lord Mayor of Bradford at the grand opening of their new superstore on the 10th August 1983. **Above**: Abdul Kader and the Lord Mayor of Bradford at the grand opening of Bombay Stores. **Right**: The Lady Mayoress learns the art of wearing a sari.*

however due to that firm's decline it became necessary for Mr and Mrs Kader to travel further, dealing with suppliers based in the Midlands and London.

As the business began to flourish, the customer base grew to include people from outside the Bradford area. This prompted the importation of different products, not only to satisfy the growing demand, but also to widen sales opportunities in order to increase profitability.

For sixteen years the man and wife team served the Asian community in their Bradford heartland, selling Lancashire cottons and muslins to Yorkshire Muslims intent on maintaining the colourful and modest dress codes decreed by their religion. As the British textile industry entered its sad decline the Kaders automatically turned to their homeland of India for supplies of fabrics and speciality-embroidered silks for the shop now trading as Bombay Stores.

The 1970s saw a natural growth in the Asian fashion fabric market within the UK; this helped the business to prosper almost effortlessly. The initially small shop was extended backwards to accommodate the growing range of products on offer.

After son Saleem joined the business in 1983, Bombay Stores opened its Wholesale/Retail showroom on Shearbridge Road. This provided the foundation for the business to build a new identity as a major player in its industry.

With weekly turnover then around £5,000 Saleem had seen the potential of wholesaling to similar outlets serving Asian communities throughout the North. The family bought the 15,000 square feet disused garage which today houses their superstore. This enterprise now caters for an eclectic clientele ranging from those seeking bargain prices to those looking for top quality materials, both of which are supplied by Indian and Japanese producers. The former will produce a fifty yard run to order, while the more industrialised Japanese would baulk at any order less than 1,000 yards.

The Kaders expansion of the eighties had been funded by the Leeds branch of the Bank of India which operates on a different system of collateral to English banks.

The early 1990s saw a change in the trend of Asian fashion as shopping now began to be seen as a leisure activity by the Asian population. This resulted in certain layout changes being introduced in store to heighten the look and appeal of the shop. In 1994 building a new wholesale premises behind the store allowed the retail side the extra space it needed.

Top and below: The familiar sight of a busy Bombay Stores.

The sale of textiles, garments, music and musical instruments, jewellery, Indian cooking utensils and luggage would soon amount to some £6 million a year.

Recognising that Bombay Stores was considered an experience by most customers the company decided to add value to its offerings by setting up a food outlet which provided customers with drinks and Indian food. The speciality being its famous Biryani.

In 1999 as a result of the company's continuing success and the need for larger wholesale premises, the current wholesale showroom was built in Woodhead Road, Bradford.

Five years later, in 2004, came the grand opening of the £1.5 million 35,000 sq ft extension to what had become the UK's largest Asian department store, bringing the company's total warehouse space to 80,000 sq ft.

The massive expansion would create up to ten new jobs at the company.

By then Bombay Stores was being run by the next generation of the family: brothers Saleem and Vaseem, responsible for wholesale and retail respectively.

Bombay Stores' business success to date has been achieved through a variety of factors: brand building, consistency of trading standards, the family business concept and employing the right people. The owners have always thought big, been ambitious - to lead the market, to excel, and be the best - and always tried to make balanced decisions.

In addition the business has always taken a long term view of its dealings with customers. Excellent customer service is the way in which the business has encouraged, gained and retained loyalty.

Nothing in business however stands still. New ways of developing the business will be required if it is to maintain its position, and indeed grow further. One such move is in diversification with investment in Perfect Occasions, the trading name under which English bridal fabrics are sold to the wholesale market.

Another area with growth potential is international distribution: in which a range of craft trade products are delivered direct to the customer straight from the source. The crafts distribution business already has a global reach, and the company will continue to build on this foundation in order to secure a place on the world stage.

Now an integral part of Bradford's long history Bombay Stores aims to grow the wholesale trade through identification of suitable markets within Europe whilst also increasing its market share within the UK.

It certainly pays to start your journey on a bus!

Top left: The opening of Bombay Stores Wholesale Warehouse, pictured above left. *Below:* A bird's eye view of the Bombay Stores site on Woodhead Road.

According to Saleem at the time of the opening 'I have long dreamed of this warehouse, although we had to wait for the right time and the right site. Fortunately, this adjacent site means we can keep the whole of Bombay Stores in one place and, with the wholesale business going into the new facility, more space is now available for the shop to expand. This is an exciting time for Bombay Stores and should secure our employees' jobs for years to come.'

Today, although retail sales are the flagship of Bombay Stores operations they in fact account for only 30 per cent of sales – wholesale amounting to the remaining 70 per cent of turnover. Though sales may have been historically aimed at Britain's Asian communities these days 40 per cent of sales are to Britain's indigenous population.

Meanwhile new commercial challenges mean more changes in the future. Home dressmaking is in decline, and with it the demand for fabric shops generally. On the other hand business enterprises aimed at the 'Asian trade' has become increasingly competitive as it has become flooded with new businesses.

SLI Lighting
An Illuminating Past and a Bright Future

The year 2007 saw a major shake up in the world of lighting and electrical products when Havell's, an Indian company, paid 227 million Euros to acquire another international company, the SLI Sylvania Group. Though SLI Sylvania's own global headquarters are in Frankfurt, Germany the name is a familiar one in Otley Road, Shipley. The company has local roots there going back for many decades.

The firm of Viking Lamps was founded in 1948 by Messrs Daniels & Bastow. The business reclaimed old fluorescent tubes. Fluorescent lamps were still quite expensive and re-pumping was economically viable especially with post-war material shortages.

Viking Lamps moved into the Rosse Works premises in Moorhead Lane near Saltaire roundabout during the late 1950s. The building was originally the workshop for repairing trams. The firm traded here as Fluorescent Starters. It later added another site at 8 Kelcliffe Crescent in Guiseley. In 1966 Viking Lamps also began working at Rosse works.

At Rosse works there was an Alexander 5ft T12 production line: other products included lamp and starter holders, 13 amp plugs and products related to the Fluorescent Starters business. A prototype T5 line was assembled at Rosse Works in the mid 1960s. Daniels and Bastow later built the Saltaire Road premises for the fluorescent equipment during 1966, leaving the metal pressing and plastic mouldings at Rosse Works.

Over stretched finances however led to Viking being taken over by Endura Lamps in 1967.

Endura Lamps, under Allenby Rivlin, was based at Low Lane Horsforth. After the takeover of Viking additional factories were added at Wyke and Apperley Bridge.

The Endura Lamps company was founded in 1953 by Allenby Rivlin in Leeds to manufacture fluorescent lamp fittings. His previous business was selling miniature lamps, mainly for the motor trade. The company traded from Meadows Lane until 1961, but by 1966 the company had moved its base to Horsforth Mills, Low Lane, Horsforth.

*Top: Rosse Works, home to Viking Lamps in the late 1950s. **Left:** Horsforth Mills, the new base for Endura Lamps in 1966.*

In 1971 another very large old mill, previously Martins Dyers and Cleaners, alongside the canal at Apperley Bridge was leased and used for equipment building, mainly a new high speed plant for fluorescent lamp manufacture. The other manufacturing operations from Horsforth and Rosse Works were also moved there during 1972. This company was called Viking Lamps Developments.

Endura was over ambitious with plans for the high speed fluorescent line designed in house and installed into Apperley Bridge by early 1975. Although the line was beginning to produce at around 1,500 lamps per hour, competitor Thorn was already at 3,000 and using far fewer operators. At this time Endura employed about 750 people around West Yorkshire. The company results deteriorated in the early 1970s. By late 1975 Endura reported losing £418,000 in six months and in December all 500 employees were to be made redundant. But it was not to be the end.

GTE was a major US corporation with manufacturing interests in a wide range of electronics, precision materials and lighting. The origins of its Sylvania brand went back to 1901 and the Merritt Manufacturing Co. of Middleton, Massachusetts which repaired burned out carbon filament lamps. Sylvania now ordered lamps from Endura to keep the operation open until Sylvania could buy it – which they did for £1!

At the time of the purchase the European Lighting Division of GTE Sylvania consisted of the Erlangen, Germany and Tienen, Belgium factories and a joint venture with Thorn called SIVI in Italy. Endura became an integral part of the lighting division.

The company had grown from the one-man operation selling car lamps to motor garages from a suitcase to a company alleged to be worth £300k in a few years, and had just formed a public company with the backing of merchant bankers Keyser Ullmann.

Endura was a major customer of Viking, taking a large proportion of its output.

An old textile mill in Wyke was purchased around 1969 and an incandescent lamp manufacturing plant, then called Endura Viking Lamps, was set up.

In 1969 the board of Endura Viking Lamps consisted of Allenby Rivlin, Chairman, E. Newman, Sales and Marketing, Geoff Eastman (a nephew of Rivlin), Production Director and Alderman W Snape as Finance Director. Frankie Vaughan the pop singer was an investor in the company and allegedly related by marriage to Allenby Rivlin.

Top: The old textile mill in Wyke purchased circa 1969 where Endura Viking Lamps was to set up. ***Above left:*** *Apperley Bridge, occupied by Endura's high speed fluorescent line in 1975.* ***Below:*** *GTE Sylvania's Erlangen, Germany site.*

This was the time of the Energysaver T8 lamp which was later produced on the high speed line in Erlangen. In Wyke there was more focus on special types of incandescent and in 1977 plans were begun for outer jacketing of high pressure mercury lamps using arc tubes from Sylvania.

In 1979 GTE purchased Claude SA in France from ITT and as a result acquired an HID plant in Reims. In 1980 line four at Wyke, the high wattage HID finishing line, was transferred to Reims. Later line three went to Lyons with the US built rotary aluminiser. Wyke was closed at Christmas 1980 and the remaining staff moved to Shipley. The site at Shipley was very cramped and operating with a remote warehouse added to the problem.

Approval was finally given for a new plant at Charlestown near Shipley and work began in 1980.

Production now included many reprographic lamps for Rank Xerox, replacing lamps sourced in the USA. Xerox proved to be one of Shipley's most demanding customers.

In 1983 sodium arc tubes went into production using equipment mainly built in the USA. The arc tubes were sent to Reims for outer jacketing. Shipley took over assembly of HID fixtures from Tienen. They were originally assembled in Erlangen. A team under Brian Cranmer spent time in Tienen familiarising themselves with the assembly operations. This was a big departure from lamp making and saw Shipley staff working with the main fixture factories at Linolite, Malmesbury and Concord, Newhaven.

1985 saw the start of compact fluorescent lamp production in Shipley. The CF-S line was built by Osram in Augsburg, Germany. GTE made a deal with Osram to produce S (single bend) lamps to their design rather than the Philips type and to do this agreed to build a line for GTE. They assumed that it would be installed in the USA, where Osram had then no market, and were surprised when the destination turned out to be Shipley.

As part of their training many Shipley production and engineering staff spent long periods in the Osram plant in Augsburg. The opening of the line was a major publicity event for Shipley and was attended by the Lord Mayor of Bradford.

Top: Shipley production and engineering staff in Augsburg. Above: Brian Simpson and Brian Cranmer by the T5 line at Saltaire Road in 1982. Left: The company's T5 automount in late 1982.

assembly in Sri Lanka. During 1994 feasibility studies were carried out to bring the assembly 'in house' at Shipley. An unusual case of assembly work coming back from a third world country. By 1995 assembly had started in Shipley, though not without major teething troubles. Many Shipley staff still carry the scars.

Philips Lighting introduced its first incandescent shaped compact fluorescent lamp in 1997 and Norman Scoular set Shipley the task of developing their own within 6 months. The product was named Ambience and production started June 1998.

With the CF-S line well established and doing what had been expected it was logical that a CF-D line (for double bend lamps) would follow. This time the decision was to build two lines in the US, one for Shipley and one for the plant in Montoursville. The line became a major co-operation project with fights over metric versus imperial standards.

However, in 1993 the UK company was sold, along with the rest of the non-US parts of GTE Sylvania, to venture capitalists led by CVC. Norman Scoular was recruited to head the buyout team and became Chief Executive of the new company. Shipley saw little change except that Product Marketing for Compact Fluorescent was set up at Shipley.

Late in 1994 Shipley developed an 'Energysaver' lamp. This would be one of the first really small fluorescent lamps to be offered as an incandescent replacement.

Sylvania's later Mini-Lynx compact fluorescent lamp was designed and built by a Swiss company with

CVC sold SLI to Chicago Miniature Lighting under Frank Ward in 1997. Norman Scoular and his team were part of the deal, but Norman's tragic death in the Swissair Flight 111 crash in September 1998 was a major blow.

The first big investment at Shipley under CML was for the triple compact line from Chi Long Machinery Co. in Taiwan.

Today, as the newest part of the Havell Group, the future of SLI Lighting looks even brighter than ever.

Top left: Preparing for sodium arc tube production in 1983. Below left: The S line at SLI. Below: SLI Lighting's Otley Road, Shipley premises.

Provident Financial over the years

ounded in 1880 by Joshua Kelley Waddilove, Provident Financial has been a part of Bradford's history for over 120 years and whilst many elements of the company have changed dramatically over this period, the fundamental principles have remained the same.

Provident Financial is a consumer lending company particularly specialising in home credit - a system of responsible lending whereby local agents lend small, short-term, unsecured loans to people from all walks of life, delivering the cash to their homes and calling back every week to collect the repayments. This has been the main business ever since the very first days of Provident back in 1880.

Joshua Waddilove was born in 1840 into a Puritan family and grew up with a strong sense of social duty and conscience. After attending Bradford Grammar School he went to work for an insurance firm, collecting money from house to house. It was in this role that he gained an insight into the needs of Bradford's working-class families.

By the time he was forty, Joshua Waddilove had progressed within the insurance company and was able to support his family with cash to spare. Joshua decided to use this spare cash to help feed and clothe struggling families and he did this by developing a system of issuing 'checks'. In those days, he knew that if he gave cash to needy families the money may well be spent unwisely; alcoholism was a big problem during that period. So, he decided to give checks to

the neediest women which could be exchanged at certain local shops for items such as coal, clothing and food.

Quickly word spread, but rather than be given 'checks' as charity, the women told Joshua they would prefer to take the checks as a loan and repay him in affordable instalments of just a few pence each week. This system fitted in very well with the self-help philosophy of the Victorian era, and very quickly became so popular that Joshua needed to employ agents to collect the repayments. He was attracting so much business to the local stores that he was able to pay them a discounted rate to settle accounts, and in a short space of time Joshua's unique form of economic aid had become a small business. He called his business 'Provident', meaning frugal, economical, foreseeing.

Above: A generous benefactor, Joshua Waddilove made significant contributions to Bradford Royal Infirmary, Red Cross and YMCA as well as giving his Bradford home to the blind and establishing the Waddilove Samaritan Home. Joshua also donated a significant amount to education in Africa and received a knighthood for his charity work.
Below: The relationship between agent and customer has always been at the heart of Provident and 127 years on, remains largely unchanged. For instance, customers still like the simple collection book showing exactly where they are with their payments.

By 1910, the business had become Provident Clothing and Supply Co. Ltd, with 85 branches nationwide, more than 3,000 agents and a turnover of nearly £1,000,000. The company continued to expand and by 1920 Provident moved to larger offices on a corner site in Westgate. This was the first of Provident's offices to be named 'Colonnade'. It was in this year that Sir Joshua died, but the business was passed down to his sons and grandsons and so remained within the family.

As with any business, Provident faced numerous obstacles during the years of the Second World War. Many men who worked for the company enlisted in the army, whilst many women had to commit to war work. The company, however, managed to adapt, turning the basement of the building into an air-raid shelter and giving staff additional responsibilities with roles such as fire wardens. Provident also contributed to the war effort by donating £50,000 to the Ministry of Aircraft Production as well as buying a Spitfire for the Royal Air Force. The Spitfire, named Provident, served for 18 months before being used as an operational training aircraft.

Top: After starting out in a tiny, first floor office, the scale of this building shows just how much the business had developed since its inception. Left: 'Provident', the Spitfire bought by the Provident Clothing and Supply Company in 1940 and a plaque commemorating the wartime gift.

During the 1950s, things continued to improve for Provident. The company regained some normality after the war years and the business grew steadily. Provident joined the rest of Bradford and, indeed, the country in celebrating the coronation of Queen Elizabeth II on the 2nd June 1953.

In 1955, Provident held a party of its own, celebrating the seventy-fifth anniversary of the company. Employees from all over the United Kingdom attended a banquet held in Harrogate, hosted by Gordon Waddilove, Chief Executive, and Ernest Waddilove, Chairman.

1962 saw the biggest change to date in the history of Provident as the company ceased being a private, family business and was floated on the London Stock Market, under the new name of Provident Financial plc. Whilst Gordon Waddilove remained at the helm, many changes were to follow for the company. Shopping vouchers were introduced and people could have credit over a period of 50 or 100 weeks, rather than the 20 week limit that had previously stood. The Bradford skyline was also poised to

Top: An important part of the community, Provident took an active part in coronation celebrations. *Above: Staff from all over the country gathered in Harrogate to celebrate 75 years of Provident.*

change when plans were drawn up for a new, modern head office to be built on Sunbridge Road to accommodate the enormous growth of this new plc. In 1967, the new Colonnade opened its doors to Provident employees.

As the contemporary head office suggested, Provident was keeping up with the modern world, not just in terms of architecture but also technology. In 1972, Provident installed a new computer centre, with a computer faster and more advanced than any they had had in the past. There were just five main roles for the computer and it had to be manned at all times. The computer was extremely delicate and had to be kept in carefully controlled and monitored conditions. This meant that the air had to be conditioned and dust free, special suits had to be worn in the centre to limit the amount of dust brought in and visitors could only see the centre through glass walls.

The strength of the UK and Ireland home credit business has led to international expansion, with Provident now offering home credit as far afield as Central and Eastern Europe and Mexico. The success of this expansion has led to Provident acquiring new premises in Leeds city centre from which to run the international side of the business. In 2006 Provident has just over 4 million customers, almost 40,000 agents worldwide and a loan book of over £2.2 billion.

Top left: *Contrasting with the predominantly Victorian industrial buildings surrounding it, the tall, white office building is still a prominent feature in Bradford today.*
Left: *Frank Wood, who retired from the company in 2006 after 41 years of service, was one of the first employees to work in the new computer centre.*
Above: *From its humble beginnings in Victorian Bradford, Provident has spread internationally. Warsaw is the home of the Provident head office in Poland.*

Whitaker & Co (Denholme) Ltd
Windows of Opportunity

Today the name Whitaker & Co (Denholme) Ltd is synonymous with high performance timber windows. These offer 'tailor-made' solutions to builders' problems – even in the Antarctic, in buildings used by the British Scientific Survey Team.

Whitaker and Company was founded by Esau Whitaker in 1900. He set up in business as a joiner, builder and undertaker at the Old School, Edge End, Denholme.

Esau's three sons eventually joined him: Harry, the eldest leaving school at 14 in 1916, Jack in the 1920s and Fred, after attending Keighley Grammar School, in 1930. Fred took charge of administration and buying, leaving Harry controlling manufacturing, whilst Jack looked after sales.

By the early 1930s more electric power was needed to meet increasing mechanisation. However, the Electricity Board could only supply the outskirts of the village, and so land at Denholme

Above: Founder Esau Whitaker. *Below:* A very early staff photograph. *Below right:* The second generation of the family, from left: Mr Jack Whitaker, Mr Harry Whitaker and Mr Fred Whitaker.

Gate was bought from the local mill owner, Garnett Foster and a new factory was built in 1933. All four walls of this original structure have now been pulled down for subsequent extensions, but the factory was the foundation for the present complex. Soon afterwards, Whitakers offered one thousand pounds for one of the fields adjoining the factory. The farmer was asking only twice that amount for his whole property and so the company bought the lot.

In the course of the second world war many of the workforce, including Fred, were drafted. The firm's premises were taken over by the Admiralty. It used the buildings for storage, whilst the company moved its manufacturing operations back to the Old School, which had fortunately been retained. Whitaker's contribution to the war effort was to make ammunition boxes, life rafts and army barracks.

At about this time, after only a short retirement, Esau died and fittingly the company made his their last coffin. The firm began rationalising its other products too, so that today only windows and external doorframes are made.

After the war, the plant moved back to Denholme Gate and the firm played its part in the nation's massive re-housing

Winnard and Carol's husband Antony Cam joined the board – Geoffrey as Non-executive Director, Antony as Technical Director. This ensured the family tradition continued into the fourth generation.

Meanwhile, the firm has found time to take an interest in the wider community. The family was always supportive of the Denholme Branch of the Royal British Legion and the local Anglican Church, which was a next door neighbour until 2000. The firm has also played an active part both regionally and nationally in the National Federation of Builders (NFB) and the British Woodworking Federation (BWF). Their commitment to these organisations was demonstrated when Jack became president of the BWF in 1962, and some years later in 1995, Keith was elected as president of the NFB Yorkshire region.

Whitaker & Co has demonstrated its technical superiority by helping to pioneer new techniques in timber conversion and drying, a process known as 'greensplit'. The company was also a major influence and founder member of the BWF Timber Window Accreditation Scheme and this scheme has been so successful that it can now boast the prestigious BSI Kitemark.

Today, confident in the fact that timber is the only natural renewable material for manufacturing windows, Whitaker & Company continues to flourish despite competition from manufacturers using other materials.

programme. In 1954 it became a limited company with a well-respected name within the joinery industry. The present office block and some extra factory accommodation were built and yet further expansion followed.

Fred remained a lifelong bachelor but the firm had been joined by Jack's two sons, Rex and John, and Harry's son Keith. Sadly, John died in 1963, aged only twenty-three after working less than four years. Shortly afterwards, Esau's sons died in quick succession, Fred whilst still in service in 1969 and Harry and Jack following short retirements.

Rex, as Chairman and Managing Director, and Keith managed the company jointly from then until Rex's death in 1983. His widow, Joyce, then joined the company as Chairman with Keith as Managing Director for a prosperous six year spell.

In 1989 Joyce retired and, following restructuring, Keith took over as Chairman and Managing Director. The early 1990s were difficult years due to the severe recession but despite this the company improved quality to such an extent that it achieved the coveted BS5750 (BS EN ISO 9001).

Keith's daughters Carol and Joy joined the company in 1982 and 1990 respectively. Following Keith's retirement from the board in 2005 Joy was appointed Chairman and Carol, Managing Director. At the same time Joy's husband Geoffrey

Top left: At work in the 1950s. Far left: Rex and Joyce Whitaker, 1964. Left: A selection of Whitakers products on display in the early days. Below: An aerial view of the works in 1971.

The Open Road with Dickinson Caravans

For many of us our leisure time is spent lazing around the house apart from an occasional trip into the countryside. However for one Bradford family providing all year round breaks is a way of life. And thanks to them thousands of satisfied customers are able to get away for weekends, indeed whole weeks, taking their own holiday homes with them.

Caravans are of course not new. The word itself comes from the 15th century Persian word 'karwan' meaning a group of travellers. The modern sense of the word however dates from the 19th century when gipsy caravans became a common sight and the word transferred itself from meaning the collection of travellers to the vehicles they travelled in.

Many Victorian folk must have envied the gipsy life style and thought they would like to emulate it themselves.

The first purpose-built touring caravan, The Wanderer, was produced to the design of Dr William Gordon Stables in 1885.

Naturally those early touring caravans were drawn along by horses. It would take the

Top: Founders Herbert and June Dickinson.
Below: The first day of opening for Dickinsons in 1976. Right: A family picture from 1982, from left: Herbert, June and son Alan.

development of the internal combustion engine to ensure that the age of the car also became the age of the caravan.

Today anyone one from Bradford looking for a caravan will put Dickinson Caravans base on Canal Road at the very top of their list. Three decades ago however those with an interest in caravanning might have been scratching their heads over where to buy a good caravan. Thanks to those efforts of one family of keen caravanners however that puzzlement was soon to end.

Dickinson Caravans was founded on 21st June 1976 by Herbert 'Bert' Dickinson together with his wife June and their son Alan.

Bert was until then a master painter and decorator in partnership with his brother in the well-known Bradford firm of Roome & Wade.

It was however Bert's wife June who was the family caravan expert. June Dickinson was already in the caravan retail business. She bought, renovated and re-sold her first caravan from the driveway of her home in Rawdon, little

was perfectly placed to be highly visible to commuters travelling to and from Shipley each day.

Within a few years the site, open seven days a week, would be able to boast up to 40 new caravans and more than 120 second hand ones on display at any one time. By 1982 an extension showroom would have to be built to the main building in order to display the many accessories on offer - part of the business built up by Alan Dickinson.

In 1991 the company took possession of some nearby premises, to use for servicing, fitting and repair work.

Sadly Bert Dickinson died in 1996, his wife June and son Alan however continue to run the business as a family concern.

Today Dickinsons Caravans Ltd offers customers a unique level of service, quality and choice – and the chance to truly savour the freedom of the road.

realising that a leading firm of caravan dealers was in the making. Alan decided to join his mother and father straight from school in opening the new company selling both caravans and accessories.

June had always had an interest in caravans from being a young girl. Immediately after the end of the second world war her father, an engineer, had built a caravan out of wood and aluminium at the rear of the family home in Undercliffe.

Alan followed in his grandfather's footsteps when he built a miniature caravan in 1979: the miniature was put on display some years ago when the company had a trade stand at the Bradford Experience held at the Richard Dunn Centre at Odsal.

Meanwhile back in 1976 there was just one full-time member of staff, Peter Walker, who is still with the company, and two part-time staff. Today, such has been the growth of interest in caravanning that there are 17 full-time members of staff and several part-time workers.

The premises were previously railway sidings so had to be redeveloped before the official opening on 5th February 1977, more than six months after the formal creation of the business. Though much hard work went into preparing the site, that effort was well rewarded, not least since the site

Top: The rear of the company's Canal Road site in 1982.
***Above left:** Coronation Street's Len Fairclough, pictured at The Northen Caravan Show in Leeds' Queens Hall alongside the miniature caravan built by Alan Dickinson in 1979.*
***Below:** Dickinson Caravans site, 2007.*

Henry Lewis - Safe and Secure

When it comes to security products one name stands out: Henry Lewis & Son Ltd now based on the Bolling Road industrial estate. Today the company produces steel security shutters and grilles, as well as many types of railings, gates and other custom made steel fabrications.

TELEPHONE - BRADFORD 5842

HENRY LEWIS & SON
BOWLING WIREWORKS
ELLINTHORPE STREET,
WAKEFIELD ROAD
BRADFORD, Yorks.

MAKERS OF ALL KINDS OF WIRE WORK
MACHINE, WINDOW & BELT GUARDS A SPECIALITY

Despite its very modern products the firm's history however goes back to the Victorian era.

In 1864 the original Henry Lewis, the present Managing Director's great grandfather, received his indentures in York for his apprenticeship in wire working.

Moving to Bradford, in 1878 he set up in business in Prospect Street off Wakefield Road. There everything was handcrafted: wire mesh was latticed together with fine wire without welding.

Top: A Henry Lewis & Son business card from the 1940s. Right: Charles Lewis, son of the founder. Below: Francis Lewis (left), grandson of the founder and his son Roger outside the company's Wibsey Bank premises circa 1960.

The business made and wove its own wire mesh on a handloom, manufacturing a variety of products from sieves to church window grilles – many of the latter still in place.

After the second world war Francis Henry Lewis joined his father Charles Lewis in the family business, and in the early 1950s his sister Mary's husband Jack joined them. Sadly however Jack was to die only a few years later.

By then the business had moved into premises in Ellinthorpe Street off Wakefield Road, ground floor premises of around 250 square feet.

Safety was now becoming an issue, and machinery that had previously been left unguarded now required specialist attention which Henry Lewis & Son delivered all over the district.

In the mid-1950s the company moved to premises in Holroyd Hill, Wibsey. Unhappily it was full of leaks, with a flagged

By 1973 the foreman, Charles Hudson, had died and Roger took over with the help of Graham Hall, one of the directors. That same year Roger's daughter Suzanne, now a director herself was born. Work progressed with contracts for British Steel and the National Coal Board.

By the end of the 1970s the market for machine guards was declining, although it would be ten years before the company wholly switched to security products.

After a fire in Upper Castle Street that almost saw the end of the company, a piece of land was purchased in the mid-1970s from Bradford Council in the Ripley Ville area. By 1978 the first part of what would become 4,500 square feet of factory space was built.

stone floor and hardly room to turn without tripping over something or someone.

Both Charles Lewis and his son Francis died in the early 1960s missing the big changes of the following years.

By the 1960s machine guards were the company's main product; gas welding was now in place: intricate guarding for carpet loom manufacture was the main source of income. David Crabtree & Son of Dick Lane being the largest customer. Its products went all over the world with Henry Lewis guards covering them.

The company was run for the next few years with a foreman and new directors. The present managing director, Roger Lewis, started to learn the trade in 1962 after leaving school. He had to start at the bottom, making tea and weaving wire mesh, crimping wire and threading it into the loom in the same way cloth is woven.

In the late 1960s new premises in Upper Castle Street were acquired.

Meanwhile many manufacturers were buying mesh and making their own guards, so a distributorship was set up through which welded mesh was sold the trade. By the mid-1980s at the height of that trade over 100 tonnes of welded mesh were being sold annually.

By then however, roller shutters had been introduced. Originally the company had bought them in for resale, but an extension built in 1988 made manufacturing possible. Riots in Leeds and Bradford changed the face of the business: demand for roller shutters rose dramatically.

In the early 1990s a new product was introduced: 'Excalibur' – a retractable grill with a better-looking finish, at a very affordable price.

The welded mesh warehouse was cleared and a powder coating plant installed with cleaning tank and drying facilities. Another extension was built to house a steel-rolling mill and an injection-moulding machine. Staff numbers grew to almost 40.

Today Graham Hall has retired after 40 years with the company. Roger Lewis still runs the business but expects to soon hand over the reins to daughter Suzanne.

Top: Roger Lewis (left) at work in the early 1960s.
Above: An elevated view of the shop floor in the 1980s.
Right: An example of security grilles and shutters manufactured by Henry Lewis & Son.

Christeyns UK - A Green Future

Belgium-based Christeyns Group has subsidiaries all over Europe. The Bradford part of the Christeyns' story goes back to 1874 when the firm of John Hellewell & Sons Ltd. was set up. From premises in Walker Terrace, off Wakefield Road, the business dealt primarily in oils used for lubrication and processing in the textile industry.

The textile trade declined badly throughout the 1950s. In 1963, tired of 'going it alone', Hellewells amalgamated with two other companies. One of them, Gledhills of Scoresby Street in the centre of Bradford, was in the same line of business and it was their premises that became the base for the new company, Oils & Soaps Ltd.

The other new partners, Salmon and Nephew, were soap merchants. That company turned tallow (fats from animals) into soaps and auxiliary products also required by the textile trade. It was a thriving concern, operating from a factory in Valley Road, but the neighbours found the tallow smell offensive and environmental regulations obliged it to close it down.

Fortunately, Salmons' managing director was a good friend of his opposite number at John Collier, who agreed to make soap for him. Collier's is still in business today.

By the 1970s with the textile industry no longer requiring its products Oils & Soaps switched to making detergent-based cleaning materials. The Company obtained contracts for detergents to clean all Bradford schools and for supplying the '5-Minute Car

*Above left: Founder, John Hellewell. **Above right:** David Hellewell, former Managing Director of Oils & Soaps. **Below:** A view inside Christeyns laboratory.*

Wash' company's branches throughout the country. The raw materials were bought in and mixed and blended at the factory which grew to keep pace with the rapidly expanding chemical industry.

In 1971, the construction of the Bradford Inner Ring Road had finally been decided upon. Oils and Soaps was the first company to move out of the Scoresby Street premises, pre-empting compulsory purchase. It then purchased the present premises in Rutland Street.

The original partnership of Oils & Soaps Ltd did not last very long before David Hellewell bought out his partners and became managing director. His son Peter succeeded him so that the firm was run by its founding family until Frank Braithwaite, the present MD took over. The Company was sold in 1997 to become part of Wilton Investments Ltd.

Today the Rutland Street site contains administration and manufacturing whilst the distribution of finished goods is dealt with from the warehouse at Eastwood Street. The Company maintains a well-equipped laboratory with a technical team which provides quality control, ensuring all raw materials, processes and finished goods conform to the exacting requirements of ISO 9001:2000. There is a dedicated development team continuously investigating new raw materials and processes for all areas of the business.

The Company was bought by the Bostoen family of Belgium in 1998 and changed its name to Christeyns UK Limited. The Christeyns Group has subsidiaries in 12 European Countries with a turnover of around 100 million Euros and over 400 employees. Christeyns UK Limited continues to operate autonomously run by Managing Director, Frank Braithwaite. Investment in production plant and equipment, warehousing, and the purchase of land and properties adjacent to the Rutland Street site, together with a major refurbishment in 2001 resulted in an annual capacity of 40,000 tonnes of powder products and 80,000,000 litres of liquid products. The company now employs a staff of over 100 in Bradford across three sites, having acquired a third manufacturing facility at Prospect Street.

Over the past decade the company has continued to expand and its turnover has tripled. Although the industrial laundry sector is its main market, the company has expanded its business in the construction-products market supplying products primarily to the concrete industry under the brand name of Oscrete, and has a thriving manufacturing business supplying and distributing a range of products from wax furniture polish to water treatment chemicals.

Christeyns was very proud to achieve accreditation to the ISO 14001:2004 Environmental standard, certifying that products are manufactured with regard to the environment. This together with the company's Environmental Sustainability Programme, designed to minimise the impact of raw materials, packaging and production on the environment, has helped make Christeyns' manufacturing facility in Bradford a comfortable home for a breeding pair of kestrels who visit each year – testament to the company's 'green' credentials.

Above left: *Bagging of Oscrete products.* ***Below:*** *One of the company's fleet of arctics outside their Rutland Street premises.*

Yorkshire Building Society
The Pleasure is Mutual

Today Yorkshire Building Society, with its headquarters in Rooley Lane, Bradford, is one of the largest building societies in the UK.

The Society is a 'mutual' organisation, owned by - and run for the benefit of - its members and not outside shareholders.

In the early 1990s Yorkshire was the first building society to commit itself to remaining a mutual at a time when many others decided to become banks.

Today, wherever members live, Yorkshire Building Society is with them one hundred percent with its 131 branches and network of agencies spanning the country. The Society's Head Office, however, remains in Bradford. Yorkshire House in Rooley Lane is part of a purpose-built development and is home to over 1,000 staff. Yorkshire also has a second head office building on Filey Street, Bradford where a further 350 staff are employed. Many however will remember the Society's former head office, an eight storey building on Westgate in the city centre.

Yorkshire Building Society has grown to become one of the largest building societies in Britain. For many years it has also been one of the most cost-effective in the industry.

Above: Founder, Henry Bushell. **Below and right:** *The Society's Banking Hall (below) at Queen Anne Chambers (right).*

In 2006, it cost just 69p per £100 of assets to run the Society. This management expense ratio is one of the lowest of any building society. It is also central to the Society's policy of growing the business as efficiently as possible in order to generate enhanced benefits for members.

The earliest roots of today's Society can be traced back not to Bradford, but to Huddersfield.

It was in 1864 that the Huddersfield Equitable Permanent Benefit Building Society was established by three gentlemen who met each morning from 5am to 8am in a single room in the town. Early directors of the Society included a dentist, a shoemaker and a plumber. A 'permanent' Building Society was so-called to distinguish it from earlier building

modernised offices of the Bradford Permanent opened at Queen Anne Chambers with rubber-covered floors and ultraviolet ray glass.

The following decades would be ones of growth for building societies, especially in the years following the end of the second world war when many more ordinary folk decided to buy their homes. Yet the day of the small, exclusively local, building society was over.

In 1975 the Huddersfield and Bradford Building Societies merged in the largest marriage of two societies to that date.

Seven years later, in 1982, the Huddersfield & Bradford and West Yorkshire Building Societies merged and the Yorkshire Building Society was born!

Mergers continued in 1992 when Yorkshire Building Society joined with the Haywards Heath Building Society. The Yorkshire also merged with the Gainsborough Building Society. Both these Societies were much smaller than Yorkshire Building Society and therefore the name remained unchanged.

societies, which were wound up as soon as all its founder members were enabled to buy their own homes. Assets at the end of the first year total £4,044 13s 5d. There were six borrowers.

In 1866 the West Yorkshire Building Society was established at the Royal Hotel in Dewsbury with only two staff. Five years later it was doing so well that an umbrella and a rug were purchased for the Society's offices!

Bradford was slow to catch up, but in 1885 the Bradford Self Help Permanent Building Society was established in St. George's Hall Coffee Tavern, initiated by Henry Bushell who at the age of twenty-four became the founder of the Society and its first Secretary. Assets at the end of the first year totalled £185, with 43 members.

During its first four years of business the Bradford Permanent opened for just an hour and a half once a week, but by 1893 the Society's office was fitted with the electric light. Operations at Bradford were to remain on a small scale for some time. In 1915 the first lady employee joined the Society.

By 1923 in Dewsbury the staff of the West Yorkshire Building Society had doubled – to four. In Bradford however, things were moving on more briskly: in 1930 the

By 1999 Yorkshire Building Society's assets topped £10 billion. By 2001 Yorkshire Building Society had become the third largest mutual in Britain with assets of over £11 billion. By 2007 the Society had 1.8 million members and assets of £17.6 billion.

Top left: Bradford & Permanent Building Society pictured in the 1970s. **Above right and right:** Director and Chief Executive Derek F Roberts receives the key to the superbly equipped new corporate headquarters (right) from Mike Laycock, Chairman of Taylor Woodrow (Northern) Ltd.

H S Wood (Textiles) - Changing Times

H S Wood (Textiles) Ltd, the founding company of what has become the Wood Group of companies, was formed in 1974 by H Stephen Wood. Until then his working life had been spent in the family textile business, which due to financial problems had recently been sold to Woolcombers Ltd.

When the family company was sold a restriction was placed on Stephen Wood preventing him from trading in the speciality fibres such as mohair and alpaca which he had previously sold. As a consequence of this contractual legal limitation Stephen decided to begin trading in all types of waste. This was a practical way forward: Stephen had many connections in the trade who were very helpful, and furthermore the cost of buying waste was very small and needed little start up capital.

Over the first two years there was only Stephen Wood and Brenda Newall who did all the secretarial and office work in the new firm. 'I shall always be grateful to Brenda for her loyalty and hard work over many years' says Stephen today. Stephen was also fortunate to meet Jimmy Watson in the early days of trading; he joined the company his knowledge

and expertise being vital to the growth of the waste business. Jimmy was an outstanding character and well known in sporting circles. Tony Duckworth and Jeff Medley have also been very loyal and vital members of the company, and still remain with the firm today. Stephen will always be very grateful for the support and help of his many friends, in particular, Brian Haggas and Richard Robinson, whose advice was invaluable during the bad and the good times.

During the first six years the company expanded, doubling its profits every year. A useful new form of business tax relief had been brought in by the Labour Government enabling the business to not only expand but also significantly increase the amount of stock it carried.

The company grew and now expanded into other areas including property. Mr Wood's property holdings would eventually increase by such a degree that by the time he relinquished the post of Managing Director in 2002 he had become the owner of twelve textile mills in Yorkshire: only three however would remain as working mills the remainder either being demolished and houses built on the sites or split into smaller industrial units.

Meanwhile, in 1984, Mr Wood had bought a 50 per cent stake in DHC (Bfd) Ltd, a company which de-haired cashmere and camelhair, solely on a commission basis. The company prospered to become the largest Commission Dehairer in Europe.

Seven years later, in 1991 Wm Fein & Son Ltd, based in Holmfirth, was acquired from Elders, the Australian brewery company. The trading restriction which had been placed on Mr Wood by Woolcombers Ltd had long since expired and he was once again able to trade in cashmere, camelhair and angora, products in which Wm Fein was a leading company in the field. This company went from strength to strength before being sold to an American company in 1994. In the year in which it was sold that company's turnover was over £12 million, gaining it the Queen's Award for Export.

CASHMERE
FOR THE CONNOISSEUR

In 1996 the Wood Group purchased GBU (Northern) Ltd. This company dealt in various types of waste, but mainly in used clothing it bought from various charity organisations. With the decline of the textile trade in Yorkshire the company felt it had to diversify more into this side of the business. The original mills which supplied the waste for sorting and reprocessing by HS Wood (Textiles) Ltd were no longer in existence. GBU (Northern) Ltd now processes or sorts over 120 tons of used clothing every week.

Stephen Wood's other interests during his varied and exciting business life have included buying a hotel in Harrogate, now owned by his two sons, and also a development at Vale Royal Abbey near Chester. Vale Royal Abbey was previously the home of the Cholmondeley family, Thomas Cholmondeley becoming the first Lord Delamere. A golf course was built in the grounds and the house converted into a magnificent clubhouse along with 13 luxury apartments. A new driveway was constructed and the land on either side sold for the building of 50 houses.

Today the Wood Group based in Park View Mills, Raymond Street continues to expand its business in textile clothing and now even owns a factory in Latvia. Stephen Wood's son Richard who is now Managing Director of the various companies runs the Group. Richard travels extensively both to the Continent and the Far East, in both a buying and selling capacity. Richard states 'having accepted that certain parts of the textile trade have gone forever, I am looking at

different businesses into which we can expand. Many of the difficulties associated with business in this country are the result of the high costs of the labour force in comparison to many other countries abroad This, coupled with the enormous increases in utility costs, make the possibilities of manufacturing in the United Kingdom extremely difficult'.

Top left: Founder, Mr Stephen Wood. **Left**: H S Wood's Park View Mills. **Above:** Wm Fein & Son advertising of Cashmere from the 1990s. **Right**: Mr Richard Wood, Managing Director of H S Wood.

Bradford & Bingley - Building a Better Future

Today Crossflatts, Bingley is home to one of Britain's largest financial institutions – Bradford & Bingley plc, corporate successor to the Bradford & Bingley Building Society.

The Bradford & Bingley Building Society was formed in 1964 as a result of the merger of the Bradford Equitable Building Society and the Bingley Building Society, both of which were established in 1851.

B&B's story goes back to the years following the Industrial Revolution. In the centres of the textile industry in Yorkshire, workers left their remote cottages and came to live in clusters around the mills where there was work to be had. It began to be realised that the savings of one group could provide the loans required by another, so that buying their houses became a not unreasonable ambition for mill workers in steady employment. Many small building societies would be formed in this period with the aim of helping working folk own their own homes.

The Bradford Equitable was the second earliest Building Society to be formed in Bradford, after the Bradford Union.

Above: *The Bradford Equitable granted its first mortgage to John Abbey (pictured) in 1851. Mr Abbey a foreman weaver borrowed £300 to by a house at 11 Clayton Lane.* **Below:** *Main Street, Bingley circa 1900.* **Right:** *Bradford Equitable's Bank Street premises, 1895.*

It held its first meeting at the Mechanics' Institute in 1846, prospered steadily, and by the early 1960s, led by its chairman at the time, Walter James, had amassed assets of £52 million.

Beyond Bradford, Bingley, slightly more rural with one third of its population still engaged in farming in the first half of the 19th century, still felt the impact of the new industrialisation. There too, small groups of savers formed similar societies and, in 1871, several of these enterprises

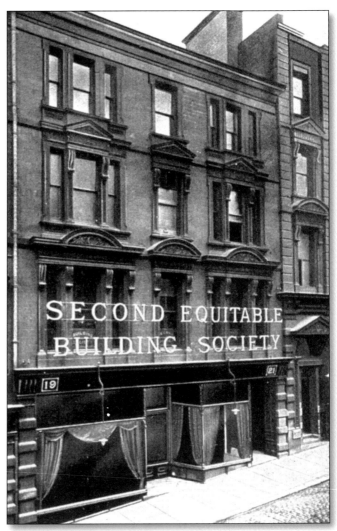

obliging investor in those wishing to better their fortunes through loans to buy their own property. And the best way to meet the challenge of the future was major change.

In July 2000 the Society's voting members overwhelmingly endorsed a proposal from the Board of Directors to convert to a public limited company. The flotation on the London Stock Exchange took place on 4th December 2000.

When the organisation began its purpose was clear: simply to build a better future for the people of northern mill towns. In 1851, it helped its very first customer, John Abbey, build a better future for himself and his family by lending him money to buy his own home. Today the B&B has changed remarkably – it has 205 branches and has more than £36 billion loaned to clients. Yet some things have not changed: the B&B is very proud of its heritage and, in the Bradford & Bingley Group, that heritage continues to shape the business and its purpose. B&B is still building a better

joined to form the Bingley, Morton, Shipley & Keighley Permanent Benefit Building Society. Many building societies featured the word 'permanent' in their title to distinguish them from temporary building societies, the latter which were wound up as soon as all their original limited number of members had paid off their mortgages.

By 1962, after similar steady growth, its assets of £41 million rivalled 'The Bradford'. The Bingley Society's general manager, Bob Gardner, wanted his society to be in the list of the top ten societies and looked for the merger with a similarly sized society that would be necessary to fulfil his ambition.

The Bradford & Bingley Building Society was first conceived in a private conversation between Messrs James and Gardner after a meeting of the Yorkshire County Association of Building Societies, hosted by the Leeds Permanent Building Society at its headquarters on the Headrow. Many meetings later the Bradford & Bingley came into being and proved to be just as good an idea as it founders had forecast.

Ten years of small mergers with other local societies left the new society looking for acquisitions on an even larger scale. Twenty years after the Bradford Bingley merger, Bob Gardner retired, having seen the society's assets increase from £30 million to an unimaginable £3,430 million.

In the decade leading up to the millennium the biggest challenge for the Bradford & Bingley was competition in the market for mortgages and savings. It prided itself on offering a safe place for its clients' savings, on being a wise counsellor to customers seeking financial advice and an

future for people – though now they can be found across the whole of the United Kingdom.

Top left: *The merger of the Bradford Equitable Building Society and the Bingley Building Society in 1964 to form the Bradford & Bingley Building Society.* ***Below:*** *Crossflatts, Bingley, Bradford & Bingley's Head Office, 2007.*

Trevor Iles - Now Then, Keep It Clean!

Today more than ever hygiene is at the forefront of the national agenda. Established in 1973 Trevor Iles Ltd of Valley Mills, Valley Road, Bradford has grown to become the region's major distributor of hygiene supplies. The firm's highly-qualified staff – trained by the British Institute of Cleaning Science, members of and qualified Royal Institute of Health & Hygiene - are committed, not merely to supplying appropriate products, but also to adding value by ensuring prompt service and specialist advice. Clients include commerce, industry, local authorities, industrial cleaners and major retail operations. Not least are those national and international businesses whose standards are set globally: standards which Trevor Iles is proud to be able meet.

Trevor Iles, joined by colleagues Jack Lumley and Kevin Dixon, founded the business in 1973 with just six staff.

A former pupil of Woodhouse Grove School in Apperley Bridge, Trevor joined the firm of WP Butterfield (Eng) Ltd in 1962 as assistant to the Sales Manager. Amongst its products the firm made galvanised tanks, cisterns and dustbins. Eight years later he had become General Manager.

In 1973 Trevor and his two colleagues established a new enterprise making refuse containers and refuse sack holders at Greenholme Mills at Burley in Wharfdale. One of the firm's earliest successes was its collaboration with Bowater-Scott to distribute large paper sacks – predecessor of today's plastic bin

Above: Founder Trevor Iles receiving the Lever Industrial (now part of JohnsonDiversey Ltd) Special Distributor Award, 1987. Below: An interior view of Trevor Iles Ltd's Valley Road showroom.

management equipment to public sector bodies, janitorial distributors and some 'end users'. Lastly Iles Floorcare sells a wide range of floor-cleaning machines. Its team of service engineers provides maintenance both on-site and in-house.

Having expanded three times on the Valley Mills site, the company is now seeking to move or rebuild. Yet despite its growth the company retains the personal touch – perhaps nowhere better emphasised than through the company's own Social Club and its annual Christmas Parties.

bags. Yet dustbins were sold too - at the rate of 150,000 a year. So solid were they however, with a ten-year guarantee, that sales inevitably fell – replaced by the larger wheeled bin we know today.

One of the company's many design-protected products which helped establish the firm's name nationally was The Knight – a vandal-proof litter bin designed by Trevor Iles and his team. Naturally however not everything was plain sailing. The firm invested heavily in PD Plastic Ltd a firm in Skelmersdale which produced plastic bins. In 1978 as result of children playing with matches the factory burned to the ground. Happily however the business was up and running again within 18 months.

Trevor Iles is very proud to be President of the British Cleaning Council. It coordinates the affairs of the industry and is responsible for industry matters at the highest level. A former chairman of the Cleaning & Hygiene Suppliers' Association, Trevor is now a Vice-President. He is also a member of the British Institute of Cleaning Science, as well as of the Chartered Institute of Waste Management.

Trevor is joined in the business by his sons Robert and Graham, and by daughter-in-law Claire. Sadly original team member Jack Lumley has now passed away. Today Trevor Iles is Company Chairman and Kevin Dixon is Managing Director. Robert Iles is Sales Director and Graham Iles Waste Systems Director.

The company's catalogue forms "a Who's Who of famous quality products". It runs from detergents and soaps, polishes and creams to hand-care dispensers, floor cleaning goods and tissues, wet and dry vacuum cleaners, brushes, protective and workware clothing. And there's an almost unlimited range of glassware for catering.

More than 3,000 separate lines are in stock.

Top left: The company's Valley Collection of free standing litterbins. *Centre:* The Knight heavy duty litterbin, one of Trevor Iles key products in the early days. *Below:* The Board of Directors from left: Mick Crane, IFC Director, Graham Iles, Waste Systems Director, Kevin Dixon, Managing Director, Trevor Iles, Company Chairman, Peter Walker, Glassware Director, Stewart Cawthraw, Works Director, Robert Iles, Sales Director.

Thanks to the dedication of its founders, and the extraordinary loyalty of its staff – at one time 11 families had members working in the firm – the business grew significantly. Today there are 70 staff.

Iles Hygiene Supplies sells a wide range of cleaning and hygiene products and equipment. Focus Hygiene Supplies, located in Sheffield, mirrors it. Additionally Iles Glassware offers a range of products to the licensed trade, hotels and restaurants. Iles Waste Systems manufactures and sells a range of waste

Gill Demolitions - Demolition Evolution

When demolition work began on Bradford's landmark theatre, the Alhambra, in 1984 it was obvious that this was not going to be a job suitable for inexperienced contractors.

A family firm, Gill Demolitions Limited, based at Progress works in Bradford's Hall Lane, provides its customers with the highest possible standard of service and advice gained from training, certification, experience and knowledge of the industry.

That successful provision of a wide range of services within the demolition, waste, haulage and plant hire business is dependent on the company's ability to continually demonstrate a commitment to providing and maintaining a highly professional, safety-conscious service which meets the customers' needs.

Founded in 1954 as a one-man haulage business by 1969 the firm had grown to having 34 lorries and 93 staff.

The driving force behind that rapid growth was company founder Brian Gill. Driving a five ton Bedford tipper, and using his home at Tyersal as a garage, office and workshop, Brian started trading as a general haulage contractor, mainly carrying demolition materials in the summer and fuel in winter.

By dint of sheer hard work, and snatching only a few hours sleep between journeys, Brian Gill gradually increased both his business and his fleet. It was not unusual for him to work all day then spend all evening in his garage doing maintenance work on his lorry to prepare it for the next day's schedule.

In those early days Brian's wife Kathleen also played an important role, running the business whilst her husband was out driving.

Hard word and a determination to be successful and please customers paid dividends. When the demolition company which hired his lorries went out of business Brian Gill decided to tender for work in his own right. With a fleet of three lorries and a Chaseside loading shovel the company moved into Dick Lane in 1958.

Top: *Founder Brian Gill (centre) is installed as chairman of The National Federation of Demolition Contractors, North East Region, January 1984.* ***Below left:*** *An early photograph of Brian Gill's Transport Manager in one of the company's growing fleet.* ***Below:*** *Early demolition work carried out by the company.*

Soon afterwards, now with five vehicles and one mechanical shovel, the company moved its headquarters nearer to home, this time to larger premises with a larger garage at Tyersal.

Five years later the firm boasted 15 vehicles, and pressure of space led to a move to former industrial premises in Mill Street in 1963. At that time the firm acquired five excavators and moved into the plant hire field as well continuing to develop its established demolition and haulage divisions.

Typically however, the company soon grew out of its latest premises and made its fifth move in 1966, this time to Usher Street.

Its fledgling days now clearly over, and now ready for further expansion, the firm migrated to a six-acre site in Hall Lane Bradford, capable of allowing the business to grow even further.

From 1985 a second generation of the Gill family began to follow in their father's footsteps with Paul, Jonathan and Sonia Gill all eventually joining the business.

Paul Gill joined the company in 1985 having graduated from university with honours in both Business Management and Transportation. He quickly adapted himself to pricing the work and the operational running of the company with total dedication.

Paul Gill's dedication continued to grow after he was given complete control of the business 1989, taking the company forward to its present position as one of the largest and well respected demolition companies in the region.

Sonia Gill completed a full Health and Safety COSH course and became the company's Safety Officer. She also

became the Safety Adviser for the National Federation of Demolition Contractors (North Eastern Region). She was later to become the first chairman of the NFDC North Eastern Region. Sonia now works independently for the NFDC as an assessor in conjunction with the CITB Training and Assessment Board.

Jonathan Gill joined the company in 2003 taking over the operational section and becoming its project manager and Company Secretary.

Today, with the emphasis on recycling, the company's six-acre site licensed by the Environment Agency as a Waste Management Site is used as a waste facility, recycling all the demolition materials and aggregates. The company achieves its target of more than 90 per cent of materials from each demolition project including recovering waste timber, brick, concrete and stone, now being reused rather than going to landfill as was once the case.

Top left: Demolition work begins on Bradford's landmark theatre, the Alhambra, in 1984. **Above:** *A 1995 Gill Demolitions truck.* **Left:** *The present and next generation, Paul Gill and son Harrison.* **Below:** *The company's new office in Hall Lane, Bradford, 2007.*

Whaleys (Bradford) Ltd - The Fabric of Time

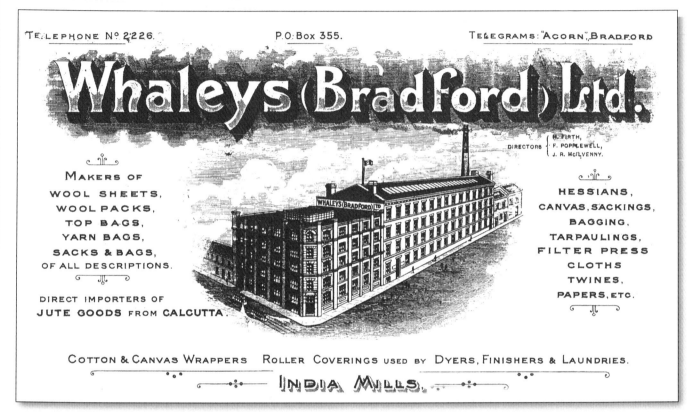

TELEPHONE Nº 2226.   P.O.Box 355.   TELEGRAMS: "ACORN" BRADFORD

Whaleys (Bradford) Ltd.

DIRECTORS { H. FIRTH, F. POPPLEWELL, J. R. McILVENNY.

MAKERS OF
WOOL SHEETS,
WOOL PACKS,
TOP BAGS,
YARN BAGS,
SACKS & BAGS,
OF ALL DESCRIPTIONS.

DIRECT IMPORTERS OF
JUTE GOODS FROM CALCUTTA.

HESSIANS,
CANVAS, SACKINGS,
BAGGING,
TARPAULINGS,
FILTER PRESS
CLOTHS
TWINES,
PAPERS, ETC.

COTTON & CANVAS WRAPPERS   ROLLER COVERINGS USED BY DYERS, FINISHERS & LAUNDRIES.

INDIA MILLS,

According to one northern trade guide customers can get 'Almost every fabric you could think of' from Whaleys (Bradford) Ltd'. Based at Harris Court, Great Horton Whaleys itself makes no claim to be able to provide every possible fabric, but it certainly offers a huge variety from natural fabrics to curtains and drapes. They also have a wide variety of bags in their range, including coal bags, garden bags and textile bags.

Whaleys can, with real justification, call itself a family firm, since Harry Jowett, who took over the reins in 1900, was the great grandfather of the present Managing Director. The firm was established in 1869 by Mr Samuel Whaley. Little is known of him now but the activities of his enterprise at that time were silk and jute weaving, with one floor taken up with processing textile sacks and bags.

At the outset the original premises were off Leeds Road in Bradford before the business moved to India Mills in Bolton Road in 1908, finally taking over its present site, Harris Court Mills in 1973.

During the first world war, weaving was suspended and silk-making abandoned. When normal work recommenced an industrial fabric section was established to furnish the textile finishing industry.

After Harry Jowett's death in 1921, the firm was taken over by his two sons-in-law, Fred Popplewell (MD) and James

*Top: A letterhead dating from 1920, showing the premises on Bolton Road. **Above left:** James McIlvenny (left) and Peter James (right) with the family founder, Harry Jowett in the picture behind. **Above right:** A family picture comprising all the directors in 1997. **Right:** The company's premises in 1994. **Top right:** Whaleys Bradford Ltd's Harris Court premises, 2007.*

Robert McIlvenny. After the last war they were joined by James' sons Harry and James Fredrick, the latter being the current Chairman, assisted by his son and Managing Director, Peter J McIlvenny, who now represent the fourth generation of the family in the business.

The company has expanded and diversified over the years. It has introduced a department which specialises in producing theatre curtains along with a range of flameproof fabrics. In addition a large fashion fabric section supplies fabric designers direct, with a separate mail order company. It is interesting to note that this includes offering silk again, after an absence of 70 years!

A sewing factory manufactures all types of bags for the textile and coal industries. Currently, over half of the company's products are exported worldwide, particularly to North America and Europe.

The management has been almost as well-known for its sporting prowess as it is for its company's products. Harry Jowett played Rugby Union for Bradford whilst James (Jimmy) McIlvenny was a professional soccer player with Bradford City. Fred Popplewell was a well-known cricketer in the Bradford League. Harry McIlvenny played amateur soccer for Park Avenue and England, whilst hockey was the sport of both James and Peter, representing Bradford and later Ben Rhydding.

In recent years Whaleys has seen a decline in the industrial fabric side of the business, especially sack and bag manufacture. There is no question that the plethora of rules and regulations regarding manufacturing emanating from the EU, combined with the severe competition from the Far East, has made UK companies unable to compete on level ground and has led to a severe downturn in the Bradford textile industry. As a result the firm was obliged to make some redundancies in that area.

By contrast the company has witnessed a dramatic expansion of the mail order side of its fabric business. Harnessing modern technology the firm boasts a first class website enabling customers across the globe instant access to information and on-line ordering. The company's computer systems have been thoroughly updated and renewed to cope with new technology. Significant strides have also been made in improving production and despatch, dramatically shortening the time period between an order being received and it being received by the customer, ensuring that Whaleys' reputation is not only maintained but enhanced.

Whaleys is a company that has seen many changes, and in fact implemented many itself in order to grow. The firm is confident of future growth and is now well placed to develop and service its markets both at home and overseas. The company continues to seek new and novel outlets for its products and is always ready to change to meet the needs of its customers in the new millennium.

Success with Stylo

Today Stylo Plc, based in Harrogate Road, Apperley Bridge, is a name known throughout Britain. The company boasts a formidable portfolio of businesses. Its growth reflects nearly a century of sound business acumen which has made Stylo the leading shoe retailer it is today.

A family run business, consolidated from three separate companies in 1935, the business was floated on the Stock Market over 70 years ago under the name of 'Stylo Boot Company (Northern) Limited'.

Yet the Stylo story is not only about the growth of a corporate business organisation but also the story of its leading light, Arnold Ziff, a classic tale of 'local boy made good'.

*Top: Founder Arnold Ziff. **Below:** A drawing of a tram with Stylo advertising. **Right:** Arnold and wife Marjorie on their wedding day, June 1952.*

Israel Arnold Ziff was born in 1927 in Chapeltown, Leeds. His family had fled from persecution by Tsarist Russia before the first world war. Despite having almost nothing on their arrival in Yorkshire, by 1930 the Stylo Boot (Northern) Company Ltd had five shops, and by 1935 it had 14. Taken collectively the family had almost 60 shops owned by three separate companies which merged in 1936.

Arnold entered the family business in 1948 after doing his National Service in the Army. Four years later the millionaire property dealer Charles Clore offered to buy the company and its then 99 branches for £400,000 – well under their true value.

The Clore offer would be declined, though Arnold Ziff would cross both paths and swords with him again.

By the late 1950s Stylo had 116 branches, with 16 in London, thirteen in Leeds, five in Newcastle and three in Bradford.

As part of the ongoing development of the group the Shellys' footwear chain was acquired in 2003. This added a further list of stores to the group portfolio in prime retail sites around the UK. This has also provided the group with an experienced design team, reactive to the market place. This has supported steady growth in the business, recently including 50 concessions nationwide.

Another development within the Stylo group is the growth of its franchise operation, which has given both the Barratts and Shellys brands several international franchise outlets mainly in the Middle East.

Stylo is also a property company with a very positive balance. Many thousands of people are employed by the company. The group turnover exceeded £230m in 2006 with net assets of £37m.

With so many properties held by the company it was no surprise that Arnold began to take an interest in property development. In 1959 another family company was created with an original starting capital of just £1,000 – Town Centre Securities. Within a short time the new company owned property worth £716,000 and was ready to raise and spend a then incredible sum of money - £2 million - on a an epoch-making new building in Leeds, the Merrion Centre.

Arnold Ziff died in 2004. Part of his life can been seen in such tangible monuments as the Merrion Centre and the hundreds of stores connected with the Stylo name. Less tangible is the lesson to be learned from his life and that of his family: hard work combined with business acumen can turn the smallest business into a commercial giant.

Today the company is led by Arnold's son Michael Ziff. Before joining Stylo in 1978 Michael was in merchant banking with Slater Walker and retailing with Debenhams. He was appointed to the board in 1980 and became Group Managing Director in 1990. Michael was appointed Group Chairman in August 2000.

Top: *An aerial view of the Merrion Centre shortly after opening in May 1964.* ***Above left:*** *The company president Arnold Ziff outside Barratts Shoes in Oxford Street, London.* ***Below:*** *Devoted husband, father and grandfather, Arnold, pictured with his family in 2002.*

The opening of the Merrion Centre in Leeds in May 1964 and its continuing growth over the following years made Arnold Ziff's name known throughout Britain. Within 13 years from its flotation Arnold had increased the value of Town Centre Securities' portfolio to a then value of £27 million, including not only the Merrion Centre but also the Rochdale Canal Company.

Meanwhile the shoe business developed rapidly and by 1964, with 150 stores nationwide, the company put in a bid to buy W Barratt and Company. After seeing off fierce competition from the mighty Charles Clore the bid was accepted and today there are over 180 Barratts stores, 190 Dorothy Perkins branded concessions and over 200 discount footwear outlets under the PriceLess fascia.

Field Packaging - Packed with Quality

Few firms last a hundred years, and even fewer get past their 150th anniversary, yet one local firm has outlived all its rivals and continues to thrive - Field Packaging is today part of a global company manufacturing high-quality consumer packaging.

A small printing partnership, Firth & Field, was set up in Northgate in 1850. Mr Firth died in 1859 but Martin Field continued in business on his own until joined by his sons, WT Field and Edgar Martin Field, trading under the name M Field & Sons. Martin Field died in 1898. A limited company was registered in 1905 becoming Field Sons & Co Ltd in 1911.

The company moved from premises in Godwin Street to Southgate in 1915.

Edgar Martin Field expanded the business from general printing to lithography and packaging. In 1926 he was joined by Mr RH Burnham, soon moving to the company's present site at Lidget Green which would be extended in the early 1930s. The Lidget Green site had been previously occupied by Scott Motorcycles, once famous for their 'Scott Sociable Three-Wheeler'.

Edgar Martin Field died in 1946 and was succeeded as Chairman and Managing Director by RM Burnham. The company continued to expand under his direction and was acquired by Reed International in 1964. Mr Burnham retired in 1973 and was succeeded by Mr CH Behrens.

In 1993, the company was part of Field Group plc which floated on the London Stock Exchange. Six years later, the business was acquired by the U.S. company, Chesapeake Corporation. Today, Field Packaging – Bradford focuses on many of the sectors it has served for the past 100 years including tobacco, whisky and confectionery. Indeed, several of its customers have traded with the business since the beginning of the 20th Century – few businesses can say that.

Field Packaging – Bradford produces a full range of printed folding cartons and spirally wound tubes for some of the World's most recognised brands. It is part of a group that employs some 5,500 people and produces packaging at over 45 locations in Europe, North America, Africa and Asia.

Top left: Martin Field.
Bottom left: The new works at Lidget Green in the 1930s. With floor space of over four acres the plant had been brought absolutely up-to-date with installation of the latest new machinery. Left: Products such as alcoholic drinks and cosmetics are often sold in worldwide markets, where packaging is judged against the highest international standards. Field Packaging provide the necessary quality assurance through the strict adherence to the most demanding quality procedures. Below: Two views of Field Packaging's Hollingwood Lane, Lidget Green site, 2007.

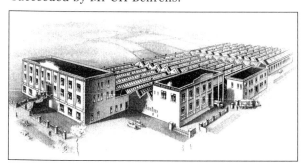

The hooter announced the end of the shift and these textile workers left Salt's Mill to make their way home for a well earned meal. Many of the people seen here spent their working lives in the industry and relaxed in the evening by listening to 'Take it from here' or the way out humour of the groons in their radio broadcasts. In the early 1950s few people owned television sets and family gatherings around the radio were commonplace. Salt's Mill was built in 1853 and at its peak employed over 3,000 men and women. The owner, Titus Salt, moved his textile base from Bradford to found the model village of Saltaire. He was a philanthropist who interested himself in the welfare of his workforce, an attitude not mirrored by many of his contemporaries. He built well appointed houses, including 45 almshouses, on a total of 22 streets on 25 acres of land, as well as the great mill that opened on his 50th birthday. The state-of-the-art mill housed 14 boilers supplying steam to beam engines that powered 1,200 looms capable of producing 30,000 yards of cloth per day. The whole development was considered to be the Utopia of West Yorkshire, far removed from the poverty which existed just a few miles down the road in the dark, satanic mills of the hymn 'Jerusalem'. Today the mill houses three galleries containing hundreds of works by Bradford born artist David Hockney.

SPORT

Over the three quarters of a century that Odsal Stadium has served the city, it has hosted various sporting events both on a regular and occasional basis. Show jumping, soccer, wrestling, speedway, stock car racing and the Harlem Globetrotters' basketball side have all been seen there. But, it is with rugby league that the ground is most associated. Nowadays, our local side is known as the Bulls. Just as Wakefield had to adapt its Trinity, so our Northern disappeared from the billboards. Those spectators who are a little long in the tooth

still hark back to the days when they stood on the terraces at Odsal and cheered on Bradford Northern as Brian Noble and Ellery Hanley stormed through the middle or, even further back, the legendary Trevor Foster. The club acquired the former quarry and tip site in 1933, building the stadium in time for the first game there on 1 September 1934. It was one of the country's largest sporting arenas and once held the record for a rugby league attendance of 102,569 when Halifax and Warrington met in the Challenge Cup Final replay in 1954.

Right: The immediate years after the last war saw a huge upsurge in attendances at organised sporting events. Football stadia were full to bursting, long queues formed outside cricket grounds to se a county match, thousands flocked to the speedway and greyhound tracks and the terraces were jammed with rugby supporters. Fans who stayed at home had been starved of their top flight Saturday entertainment, while those fighting overseas had no chance of such relaxation. Local interest was all the keener because of the success of our own rugby league side. Bradford Northern enjoyed a spell of success that saw the side sweep into three successive Challenge Cup Finals, of which they won two. This programme is the one produced for the third of these appearances, the 1949 final against close neighbours, Halifax. At one shilling (5p), it was reasonably priced; certainly if you compare it with the glossy, expensive editions supporters have to shell out for today. Even so, some people grumbled as it was double the price of the 1947 programme.

Below: The successful Challenge Cup winning team of 1949 played in front of a Wembley crowd of over 95,000, the first time that the twin towers had sold out for a rugby match. As with Northern's two previous finals,

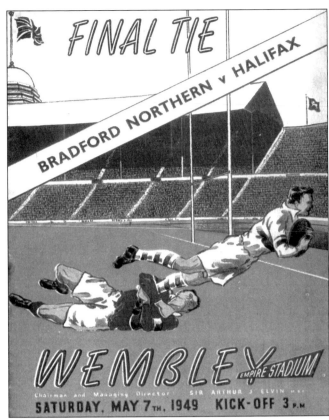

this was a low scoring game, finishing in a 12-0 defeat for Halifax. The Odsal men had lifted the trophy in 1947 with an 8-4 win against Leeds, but lost the following year's final to Wigan by 8-3. Wembley was used for the first time in 1929 and, apart from one occasion and the war years, continued to be the venue until 2000 when Murrayfield acted as host. Since then, Twickenham and the Millennium Stadium have also been used until the return to the revamped Wembley in 2007. Rugby league has continued to treasure its north country roots and despite efforts to expand the game to other parts of the country, the best sides are still to be found either side of the Pennines. Northern's line up that day was from left to right: Tyler, Kitching, Foster, E Ward, Traill, Batten, Whitcomb, Edwards, Greaves, Leake, Darlison, Davies and D Ward.

Above: The towers and chimneys of the old Canal Road power station can be seen above the stand at Valley Parade during the league match against Chesterfield in November 1954. The teams were in Division Three North during the days when the teams outside the top two divisions were placed into parallel ones on a geographical basis. It was a poor season for City, finishing three places above the bottom slot. Ivor Powell, the then manager, was still coaching football in Bath in 2006, aged 90! Coincidentally, the club was relegated to the bottom tier in 2007 after losing a match against Chesterfield. Another more terrible last day of the season game took place on 11 May 1985. Fire broke out in the 77 year old stand and 56 people lost their lives. Valley Parade was completely rebuilt by the end of the following year. The club was formed in its own right in 1903 and achieved its only major success in 1911, beating Newcastle United in the FA Cup Final.

Above: Yorkshire County Cricket was in its pomp in the late 1950s and 1960s. Championship success came its way under the surprise leadership of Bradford League veteran, Ronnie Burnet, but it was with Brian Close at the helm that the county achieved even better results. Seated centre, front row, the pugnacious Close first came to prominence in 1949 when he became England's youngest ever Test cricketer, aged just 18. He made a remarkable comeback to the Test side in 1976 when he was 45. He was also a decent footballer and turned out for Bradford City on a handful of occasions, but it was his tenacious play and captaincy on the cricket field that earned him a place in sporting history. He assumed the captaincy in 1963 and guided the side to four more championships, adding to the three won under Burnet and Vic Wilson. Dennis Brian Close, to give him his full name, also skippered the national side, but was sacked from the job in 1967 and lost the county job in 1970. He moved to Somerset and helped Viv Richards and Ian Botham blossom. The photograph was taken at Park Avenue.

Below: Can you imagine Ronaldo or any of the other pampered stars of modern football trying their stepovers and tricks on a pitch like this? Come the winter and, with every ground resembling a mudheap, the players needed sturdy boots on the end of even sturdier legs to get through 90 minutes. There were no substitutes to give the superstars a bit of a rest. It was a case of get on with it and, if you pick up an injury, go and play on the wing. In 1960, Peter Jackson was into his fifth year as the manager of Bradford City. He was Yorkshire through and through, hailing from Luddenden Foot, on the road from Halifax to Hebden Bridge. His own twin sons, Peter and David, played for the Bantams throughout Jackson's tenure. City had a good cup run this year, reaching the fifth round and knocking out Everton on the way. Burnley won the Division One championship that year and it was our bad luck to be drawn against them. Using a home tie to its best advantage, the crowd roared Webb and Stokes on to put us 2-0 up, but the visitors scored two late goals and went on to victory in the replay.

SHIPLEY ROUND TABLE

present a

CHARITY
SOCCER MATCH

SHOWBIZ XI

— V —

YORKSHIRE
C.C. XI

Odsal Stadium, Bradford

S..... ....arch, 960

NOW 2-45 p.m.

N° 8830   *Proceeds in Aid of
World Refugee Year*

SOUVENIR
PROGRAMME

2/6D.

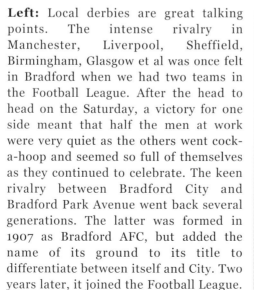

centred around a player who has featured in many quiz questions. Albert Geldard became the youngest player at 15 years and 158 days to play league football when he turned out for the club at Millwall on 16 September 1929. This photograph shows the derby game at Park Avenue in September 1967. The last of these was a goalless affair in January 1969.

Above: The rugby stadium at Odsal has been visited by many other sports. This programme for a charity event in March 1960 was produced for a soccer match between a showbiz XI and a team from Yorkshire County Cricket Club. The money raised was meant to aid refugee relief, but many of the thousands who turned up just wanted to see stars of radio, television, film and pop music. The county cricketers were less of an attraction as they could be seen on a regular basis, though there were several star names amongst their number, such as Fred Truman and Brian Close. With those two around there was little chance that the charity game would be completely without incident. At the time the game was held, Yorkshire's players were the reigning county champions. The entertainers had Tommy Steele, Ronnie Carroll, Sean Connery and Jimmy Henney in their ranks. The showbiz team changed personnel quite regularly and on other occasions called on Jess Conrad, David Frost, Jimmy Tarbuck and Des O'Connor.

Left: Local derbies are great talking points. The intense rivalry in Manchester, Liverpool, Sheffield, Birmingham, Glasgow et al was once felt in Bradford when we had two teams in the Football League. After the head to head on the Saturday, a victory for one side meant that half the men at work were very quiet as the others went cock-a-hoop and seemed so full of themselves as they continued to celebrate. The keen rivalry between Bradford City and Bradford Park Avenue went back several generations. The latter was formed in 1907 as Bradford AFC, but added the name of its ground to its title to differentiate between itself and City. Two years later, it joined the Football League. One of the club's claims to fame is

BIRD'S EYE VIEW

Aerial photography was developed during World War I as a reconnaissance measure to assist the armed forces on the ground gain an accurate picture of enemy troop movements and emplacements. It was much more reliable than trusting to the information gained from scouting parties who could only gather information from a limited area. After the war, extensive use of this art was made by government departments, both local and national, in getting a broad picture of the nature of their towns and cities that could help with future planning and building development as the country entered what it hoped would be a new dawn after the horrors of the hostilities that raged across Europe for four long years. Planners could get a better idea of the topography and current layout of roads and buildings from such bird's eye views. This photograph shows Bradford city centre in 1920. The scene is dominated by the magnificent Town Hall that was opened on 9 September 1873 by the Mayor, Alderman Matthew Thompson. It was designed by Lockwood and Mawson, a Bradford firm of architects and built by John Ives and Son, Shipley, at a cost of £100,000. It was twice extended, firstly in 1909 and then again in 1914. The clock tower still dominates the skyline today, rising some 220 feet into the air. It became known as City Hall in 1965.

Clearing some of the old, terraced property was one of the priorities after the last war as the country's programme of building work had been put on hold as everything was geared up to defeating the Nazis. With additional pressure put on local councils by the need to replace bombed out homes as well, it took some time before they caught up with the backlog. The Green Lane area, off Lumb Lane, was one of those parts of Bradford that had to

wait until the mid 1950s. Seen in 1957, the Picton Street flats had not long been completed. They looked attractively bright in comparison to the smoke blackened housing surrounding them. Tower blocks were seen as the way ahead, with several storeys of apartments housing hundreds of families in a small acreage. From this aerial landscape, Green Lane cuts across the scene, joining Lumb Lane at the right. Southfield Square is on the far side of the complex.

Seen in the swinging 60s, the aerial view follows Market Street from Town Hall Square, past Brown Muff and the Wool Exchange to Forster Square Station at the top. The Midland Hotel, on the corner of Cheapside, stands next to the station. The hotel was built by the Midland Railway Company between 1885 and 1890 and was a showpiece of its northern operations. It is of particular architectural interest, with some of the finest Victorian interiors in the city. A careful look at the roof gives an idea of the eye for detail that its designer possessed. Charles Trubshaw (1841-1917) was the son of an architect and followed in his father's footsteps for his chosen career. He joined the railway company in 1874 and, among his early work, designed Skipton Station. He was promoted from his position in the Northern Division in 1894, becoming head of the whole country's architectural plans for Midland. After a fact finding visit to the USA, he began work on the magnificent hotel in Manchester. In addition to the hotel and station here, Trubshaw was also responsible for a considerable number of others, including Leicester London Road Station.

ACKNOWLEDGMENTS

The publishers would like to thank

Bradford Central Library, Local Studies Department

Graeme Mitchell at Bradford Photographic Society

Andrew Mitchell

Steve Ainsworth

True North Books Ltd - Book List

Memories of Accrington - 1 903204 05 4

Memories of Barnet - 1 903204 16 X

Memories of Barnsley - 1 900463 11 3

More Memories of Barnsley - 1 903 204 79 8

Golden Years of Barnsley -1 900463 87 3

Memories of Basingstoke - 1 903204 26 7

Memories of Bedford - 1 900463 83 0

More Memories of Bedford - 1 903204 33 X

Golden Years of Birmingham - 1 900463 04 0

Birmingham Memories - 1 903204 45 3

More Birmingham Memories - 1 903204 80 1

Memories of Blackburn - 1 900463 40 7

More Memories of Blackburn - 1 900463 96 2

Memories of Blackpool - 1 900463 21 0

Memories of Bolton - 1 900463 45 8

More Memories of Bolton - 1 900463 13 X

Bolton Memories - 1 903204 37 2

Memories of Bournemouth -1 900463 44 X

Memories of Bradford - 1 900463 00 8

More Memories of Bradford - 1 900463 16 4

More Memories of Bradford II - 1 900463 63 6

Bradford Memories - 1 903204 47 X

More Bradford Memories - 1 903204 92 5

Bradford City Memories - 1 900463 57 1

Memories of Bristol - 1 900463 78 4

More Memories of Bristol - 1 903204 43 7

Memories of Bromley - 1 903204 21 6

Memories of Burnley - 1 900463 95 4

Golden Years of Burnley - 1 900463 67 9

Memories of Bury - 1 900463 90 3

More Memories of Bury - 1 903 204 78 X

Memories of Cambridge - 1 900463 88 1

Memories of Cardiff - 1 900463 14 8

More Memories of Cardiff - 1 903204 73 9

Memories of Carlisle - 1 900463 38 5

Memories of Chelmsford - 1 903204 29 1

Memories of Cheltenham - 1 903204 17 8

Memories of Chester - 1 900463 46 6

More Memories of Chester -1 903204 02 X

Chester Memories - 1 903204 83 6

Memories of Chesterfield -1 900463 61 X

More Memories of Chesterfield - 1 903204 28 3

Memories of Colchester - 1 900463 74 1

Nostalgic Coventry - 1 900463 58 X

Coventry Memories - 1 903204 38 0

Memories of Croydon - 1 900463 19 9

More Memories of Croydon - 1 903204 35 6

Golden Years of Darlington - 1 900463 72 5

Nostalgic Darlington - 1 900463 31 8

Darlington Memories - 1 903204 46 1

Memories of Derby - 1 900463 37 7

More Memories of Derby - 1 903204 20 8

Memories of Dewsbury & Batley - 1 900463 80 6

Memories of Doncaster - 1 900463 36 9

More Memories of Doncaster - 1 903204 75 5

Nostalgic Dudley - 1 900463 03 2

Golden Years of Dudley - 1 903204 60 7

Memories of Edinburgh - 1 900463 33 4

More memories of Edinburgh - 1903204 72 0

Memories of Enfield - 1 903204 14 3

Memories of Exeter - 1 900463 94 6

Memories of Glasgow - 1 900463 68 7

More Memories of Glasgow - 1 903204 44 5

Memories of Gloucester - 1 903204 04 6

Memories of Grimsby - 1 900463 97 0

More Memories of Grimsby - 1 903204 36 4

Memories of Guildford - 1 903204 22 4

Memories of Halifax - 1 900463 05 9

More Memories of Halifax - 1 900463 06 7

Golden Years of Halifax - 1 900463 62 8

Nostalgic Halifax - 1 903204 30 5

Memories of Harrogate - 1 903204 01 1

Memories of Hartlepool - 1 900463 42 3

Memories of High Wycombe - 1 900463 84 9

Memories of Huddersfield - 1 900463 15 6

More Memories of Huddersfield - 1 900463 26 1

Golden Years of Huddersfield - 1 900463 77 6

Nostalgic Huddersfield - 1 903204 19 4

Huddersfield Memories - 1903204 86 0

Huddersfield Town FC - 1 900463 51 2

Memories of Hull - 1 900463 86 5

More Memories of Hull - 1 903204 06 2

True North Books Ltd - Book List

Hull Memories - 1 903204 70 4
Memories of Keighley - 1 900463 01 6
Golden Years of Keighley - 1 900463 92 X
Memories of Kingston - 1 903204 24 0
Memories of Leeds - 1 900463 75 X
More Memories of Leeds - 1 900463 12 1
Golden Years of Leeds - 1 903204 07 0
Leeds Memories - 1 903204 62 3
More Leeds Memories - 1 903204 90 9
Memories of Leicester - 1 900463 08 3
More Memories of Leicester - 1 903204 08 9
Memories of Leigh - 1 903204 27 5
Memories of Lincoln - 1 900463 43 1
Memories of Liverpool - 1 900463 07 5
More Memories of Liverpool - 1 903204 09 7
Liverpool Memories - 1 903204 53 4
More Liverpool Memories - 1 903204 88 7
Memories of Luton - 1 900463 93 8
Memories of Macclesfield - 1 900463 28 8
Memories of Manchester - 1 900463 27 X
More Memories of Manchester - 1 903204 03 8
Manchester Memories - 1 903204 54 2
More Manchester Memories - 1 903204 89 5
Memories of Middlesbrough - 1 900463 56 3
More Memories of Middlesbrough - 1 903204 42 9
Memories of Newbury - 1 900463 79 2
Memories of Newcastle - 1 900463 81 4
More Memories of Newcastle - 1 903204 10 0
Newcastle Memories - 1.903204 71 2
Memories of Newport - 1 900463 59 8
Memories of Northampton - 1 900463 48 2
More Memories of Northampton - 1 903204 34 8
Memories of Norwich - 1 900463 73 3
Memories of Nottingham - 1 900463 91 1
More Memories of Nottingham - 1 903204 11 9
Nottingham Memories - 1 903204 63 1
Bygone Oldham - 1 900463 25 3
Memories of Oldham - 1 900463 76 8
More Memories of Oldham - 1 903204 84 4
Memories of Oxford - 1 900463 54 7
Memories of Peterborough - 1 900463 98 9
Golden Years of Poole - 1 900463 69 5
Memories of Portsmouth - 1 900463 39 3
More Memories of Portsmouth - 1 903204 51 8
Nostalgic Preston - 1 900463 50 4
More Memories of Preston - 1 900463 17 2
Preston Memories - 1 903204 41 0

Memories of Reading - 1 900463 49 0
Memories of Rochdale - 1 900463 60 1
More Memories of Reading - 1 903204 39 9
More Memories of Rochdale - 1 900463 22 9
Memories of Romford - 1 903204 40 2
Memories of Rothertham- 1903204 77 1
Memories of St Albans - 1 903204 23 2
Memories of St Helens - 1 900463 52 0
Memories of Sheffield - 1 900463 20 2
More Memories of Sheffield - 1 900463 32 6
Golden Years of Sheffield - 1 903204 13 5
Sheffield Memories - 1 903204 61 5
More Sheffield Memories - 1 903204 91 7
Memories of Slough - 1 900 463 29 6
Golden Years of Solihull - 1 903204 55 0
Memories of Southampton - 1 900463 34 2
More Memories of Southampton - 1 903204 49 6
Memories of Stockport - 1 900463 55 5
More Memories of Stockport - 1 903204 18 6
Stockport Memories - 1 903204 87 9
Memories of Stockton - 1 900463 41 5
Memories of Stoke-on-Trent - 1 900463 47 4
More Memories of Stoke-on-Trent - 1 903204 12 7
Memories of Stourbridge - 1903204 31 3
Memories of Sunderland - 1 900463 71 7
More Memories of Sunderland - 1 903204 48 8
Memories of Swindon - 1 903204 00 3
Memories of Uxbridge - 1 900463 64 4
Memories of Wakefield - 1 900463 65 2
More Memories of Wakefield - 1 900463 89 X
Nostalgic Walsall - 1 900463 18 0
Golden Years of Walsall - 1 903204 56 9
More Memories of Warrington - 1 900463 02 4
Warrington Memories - 1 903204 85 2
Memories of Watford - 1 900463 24 5
Golden Years of West Bromwich - 1 900463 99 7
Memories of Wigan - 1 900463 85 7
Golden Years of Wigan - 1 900463 82 2
More Memories of Wigan - 1 903204 82 8
Nostalgic Wirral - 1 903204 15 1
Wirral Memories - 1 903204 747
Memories of Woking - 1 903204 32 1
Nostalgic Wolverhampton - 1 900463 53 9
Wolverhampton Memories - 1 903204 50 X
Memories of Worcester - 1 903204 25 9
Memories of Wrexham - 1 900463 23 7
Memories of York - 1 900463 66 0